MUHAMMAD

Peace and Blessings Be Upong Him

The Best Human Being of all Time

List of Contents

List of Contents

Introduction

$\mathcal{A}$ll praise is for Allah. May the peace and blessings of Allah be upon Muhammad, upon his family, upon his Companions, and upon all those who follow his way until the Day of Resurrection.

It is often said that a writer of biographies should be neutral and unbiased, and even detached, from the object of his writing. This means that he should write a biography without interjecting into his work personal thoughts and feelings regarding the person he is writing about; furthermore, he should simply give an account of the events and occurrences of that person's life, and thus allow readers to draw their own conclusions about who that person was, and about whether he was ultimately good or evil.

And yet I cannot be neutral as I write about the one human being who is nearest and dearest to my heart: Muhammad, the Messenger of Allah (ﷺ). After all, I am not writing about a political leader who, through his ideas and efforts, helped established a country in one of the corners of the earth; instead, I am writing about the Messenger of the Lord of all that exists, about a man who was sent as a mercy to all of mankind.

While writing about him (ﷺ), I cannot be unbiased. I am not, after all, writing about a ruler who had a large retinue of servants; who owned vast treasures of gold and silver; who would come before his people wearing a crown, an expensive robe, and priceless jewels. Such was the way of countless kings throughout history, but it was not the way of the man that I write about in this book. His wealth also was vast, but it was of the spiritual, and not of the material, kind. He was and continues to be a source of constant blessings for mankind. He is Muhammad, the Messenger of Allah (ﷺ).

I am not writing about a ruler or dictator who subjugated people at the edge of a sword or at the point of a gun, a ruler who kept a firm grip on power by making his people fear him — by making them feel terrified of his very name. I am instead writing about one who was divinely protected — one whose heart Allah (ﷻ) opened, whose mistakes Allah forgave, and whose name Allah elevated. With all of that in mind, how, then, can I remain neutral?

The one about whom I write was not a confused poet, a misguided philosopher, a loquacious speaker, or an imaginative writer. Instead, the one about whom I write was the seal of all Prophets. The Angel Jibreel (ﷺ) would come to him, and revelation would descend upon him. Above the heavens, he reached the lote-tree, the farthest place any human being — or any angel, for that matter — has ever reached. On the Day of Resurrection, he (ﷺ) will be in a position of great honor; he will have his own basin, towards which countless numbers of Muslims will flock; and he will be granted what is known as the "Greater Intercession".

Would you have me hold back my emotions and keep in check my heart-rate when I am writing about the one person whom I love more than all other people combined? Would you go so far as to ask me to hold back my tears and to extinguish the flames of love I feel in my heart while I write about his life? If that is the case, then I can never do as you ask, not if you were to offer me all of the riches of this world.

I am not neutral about the subject-matter of this work because I am writing about someone who is the leader and guide of all of mankind. When I pray, I remember him because he (ﷺ) said, "Pray as you have seen me pray."[2] When I perform Ḥajj (pilgrimage to Makkah), I remember him because he (ﷺ) said, "Take from me the rites of your pilgrimage."[3] With every blinking of my eye, I remember him because he (ﷺ) said, "Whoever turns away from my Sunnah (i.e., my way, my guidance) is not from me."[4] And in every second of my life, I remember him because Allah (ﷻ) said:

﴿لَّقَدْ كَانَ لَكُمْ فِى رَسُولِ ٱللَّهِ أُسْوَةٌ حَسَنَةٌ ... ﴿٢١﴾﴾ (سورة الأحزاب: ٢١)

﴿Indeed in the Messenger of Allah [Muhammad] you have a good example to follow...﴾ *(Qur'an 33: 21)*

I am writing about a man who categorically is the best human being ever to have walked the earth. And what are the sources and reference books I used to write this book? Were they encyclopedias and history books? No. Instead, my main reference works were the book of love for the Prophet (ﷺ) that I have stored in my heart and the book of unadulterated veneration of the Prophet (ﷺ) that is inscribed — indelibly, I hope — in my memory. It is as if I am writing not with my hand and a pen, but with my nerves and my heart's arteries. And, because of my great love for the Prophet (ﷺ), it is as if the ink I am writing with consists of a mixture of my tears and blood.

---

[2] Related by Bukhari (631), on the authority of Mâlik ibn al-Huwayrith.

[3] Related by Muslim (1297), on the authority of Jâbir ibn 'Abdullâh.

[4] Related by Bukhari (5063) and Muslim (1401), on the authority of Anas ibn Mâlik.

The Story of Prophethood

Muhammad

(Peace Be Upon Him)

His Name

The name 'Muhammad' means 'the praised one'. Therefore, the Prophet's name is as much a title that describes the Prophet's qualities, as it is a name that identifies the Prophet (ﷺ) as an individual. Any noble quality one can imagine, the Prophet (ﷺ) possessed. He is divinely protected; he is the seal of all Prophets (ﷺ); he is Allah's obedient slave; he is the chosen one from Allah's created beings; and he is Allah's *Khaleel* — a *Khaleel* is more than a friend; it denotes the highest level of friendship and love — therefore, he is certainly deemed one who is worthy of being commended by Allah. And he (ﷺ) is deemed worthy of praise by people, for he is near to their hearts, merciful towards them, and blessed no matter where he is.

He is worthy of praise because his character became refined through revelation, and because his personality became polished through prophethood.

He was known by various names, each of which pointed to at least one of his noble qualities. 'Eesa (Jesus) (﷽) gave glad tidings of him to his people, promising them that a Prophet named Ahmad was soon going to be sent to guide mankind to the truth. A few of his other names are *al-'Âqib*, *al-Hâshir*, and *al-Mâhee*. *Al-'Âqib* means 'one who succeeds others', or 'one who comes after others'; the Prophet (ﷺ) was given that name because he came after all other Prophets (﷽) and because no other Prophet will come after him. *Al-Hâshir* connotes the meaning of resurrection; the Prophet (ﷺ) was given that name because, when this world will come to an end, people will be resurrected at his feet. And as for the name *al-Mâhee*, it connotes the meaning of 'erasing something'; the Prophet (ﷺ) was called *al-Mâhee* because, through him, Allah (ﷻ) erased disbelief.

The Prophet (ﷺ) was mentioned in both the Torah and the *Injeel* (the Gospel); he was helped in his mission by Jibreel (﷽); he carried the banner of honor for the Banu Luaiy clan; and he was the most honored member of the Banu 'Abd-Manâf ibn Qusaiy clan.

He (ﷺ) was rightly-guided himself; he was the best of guides for others; he was elevated in ranking by his Lord; he was thankful for all that Allah blessed him with; and he was, and continues to be, a source of countless blessings for all of mankind. May the peace and blessings of Allah be upon him, upon his family, and upon his Companions as long as stars appear in the sky, as long as birds continue to sing, and as long as the wind continues to blow.

His Lineage

*I*n terms of his lineage, the Prophet (ﷺ) was the best, from the best, from the best — all the way back to his last forefather, Adam (ﷺ). He (ﷺ) was born to parents who did not fornicate, but who instead were married. His forefathers were leaders among people, chiefs of tribes and sub-tribes. Each one of them inherited noble qualities from his forefathers. If you were to go back twenty years before the Prophet's birth, you would not find a man who possessed the noble qualities that the Prophet's grandfather, 'Abdul-Muṭṭalib, possessed. And if you went a number of years further back, you would not find a man who was nobler and better than the Prophet's great-grandfather, Hâshim. The same can be said about all of the Prophet's forefathers - 'Abd-Manâf, Quṣaiy, and every one of the Prophet's forefathers between Quṣaiy and Adam.

His Homeland

*F*rom all of the places on earth, Allah chose for His Prophet the most beloved of lands to Him — the inviolable city, the holy city, the city of pure soil, the city that was under His constant protection. Yes, the Prophet (ﷺ) was born in Makkah, the city wherein Prophets and Messengers performed Prayer, the city in which revelation came down. Moreover, Makkah was the city that contained in it the Ancient House, the Ka'bah.

It was in Makkah that the Prophet (ﷺ) was raised as a child; it was Makkah's streets that the Prophet (ﷺ) became familiar with as a boy, and then as a young man; and it was Makkah that became dearer to the Prophet (ﷺ) than all other lands. When he was forced to leave Makkah, he was going to a place where he would be honored, and yet he did not really want to leave. Addressing the city he loved the most, the Prophet (ﷺ) said around the time he was forced to leave it, "By Allah, you are the best of Allah's lands, and the most beloved of Allah's lands to Allah. And had it not been for the fact that I was forced to leave you, I would not have left."[5]

It was in Makkah that the Prophet (ﷺ) first received revelation; it was there that he first preached his message; and it was there that he and his followers congregated for the very first time.

When the Prophet (ﷺ) was forced to leave Makkah, he bid farewell to it in a beautiful manner; and when he actually left, he could hardly endure the pain of separation — the pain that one feels when one is forced to leave something that is very near and dear to one's heart.

(سورة البَلَد: ١-٢) ﴿۞ لَآ أُقْسِمُ بِهَٰذَا ٱلۡبَلَدِ ۝ وَأَنتَ حِلُّۢ بِهَٰذَا ٱلۡبَلَدِ ۝﴾

﴿I swear by this city [Makkah]. And you are free [from sin, to punish the enemies of Islam on the Day of the conquest] in this city [Makkah].﴾   *(Qur'an 90: 1, 2)*

---

[5] *Sunan at-Tirmidhi* (3860).

The Child

*T*he Prophet (ﷺ) did not descend from the heavens at the age of forty, ready immediately to begin preaching the message of Islam. On the contrary, he entered this world in the same manner that all other children (of course with the exception of Adam, Eve, and Jesus, may Allah's peace be upon them) entered it: His mother became impregnated by his father, and about nine months later he exited from her womb. Furthermore, his aging process was not accelerated for him, whereby he transformed from an infant into a forty-year old Prophet in a matter of moments, weeks, or months. No, time passed by for him in a normal fashion, and, as with all of the other people on earth, he had to go through the various stages of life — infancy, childhood, young adulthood, all the way to old age.

What was he like as a child? To put it simply, he was a child, but was not like other children. He was both innocent and born of excellent lineage, and he was at once intelligent and pure. Perhaps what distinguished him most from other children was the fact that, at every stage of his young life, he was being divinely protected by Allah. To the keen-sighted observer, Muhammad the child was being prepared for great things. Everyone who played a part in raising him — his mother; his nursemaid, Ḥaleemah (ﺭ); 'Abdul-Muṭṭalib; and Abu Ṭâlib — knew that he was being divinely prepared for a great mission in life, but what that mission was, they probably couldn't guess (except of course for Abu Ṭâlib, who had been informed by a monk about the seal of prophethood on Muhammad's back).

Divine protection didn't just mean that Allah (ﷻ) protected Muhammad (ﷺ) from physical harm; actually, it primarily meant protecting him in a spiritual sense. Thus, as a child or even as a young adult, Prophet Muhammad (ﷺ) was never known for frivolity, for lying, for having bad manners, or even for the innocent mischief-making that is common among children. He remained innocent and without a blemish to stain his character because he was being prepared to bring happiness to mankind, to bring them out of darkness and into the light. Thus he was a man, and yet a Prophet; he was a human being, but at the same time he was a Messenger; he was a slave of Allah, and yet he was divinely protected from doing wrong; he was a human being, and yet revelation descended upon him.

In historical terms, it is false to depict Prophet Muhammad (ﷺ) simply as being a leader. The leaders who have lived on earth and then died are similar in number to the hair on one's head. They had ambitions for power and aspirations for great wealth, and they achieved the trivial things they had set out to gain. Few people remember them, and even less care about them. But the Prophet (ﷺ) was much, much, much more than a leader. He was a guide and a Prophet; he came with the Book of Allah and with his own Sunnah; he came with light and guidance; he came with beneficial knowledge and righteous deeds. He focused on people's well-being not just in this life, but in the Hereafter as well; and he was concerned not just with people's physical well-being, but with their spiritual well-being as well.

Prophet Muhammad (ﷺ) was not merely knowledgeable. By the permission of Allah, he taught the knowledge he had been blessed with to others; he trained the most famous and eminent scholars and jurists of the world; he taught orators how to deliver wonderful speeches; he guided the wise and the unlearned; and he guided all people to the truth:

❨And verily, you [O Muhammad] are indeed guiding [mankind] to the Straight Path [i.e., Allah's Religion of Islamic Monotheism].❩

(Qur'an 42: 52)

Prophet Muhammad (ﷺ) was not a king who used soldiers and guards to keep a firm grip on power. He was a Prophet and Messenger sent by Allah: He was a warner and a bearer of glad tidings to every king and commoner, every free man and slave, every rich man and poor man, every Arab and non-Arab, every white man and black man.

(سورة الأنبياء: ١٠٧) ❨وَمَآ أَرْسَلْنَٰكَ إِلَّا رَحْمَةً لِّلْعَٰلَمِينَ ١٠٧❩

❨And We have sent you [O Muhammad] not but as a mercy for the ʾÂlameen [mankind, jinns, and all that exists].❩ *(Qur'an 21: 107)*

The Prophet (ﷺ) said: "By the One Who has my soul in His Hand, if any person from this Nation, if any Jew, or if any Christian hears about me and then dies without believing in that with which I have been sent, he will be among the people of the Hellfire."[6]

If we follow him from his childhood to his youth, we will find that he maintained his purity and innocence, adding to those qualities a number of other noble traits, such as eloquence, trustworthiness, good manners, and chastity. He (ﷺ) never spoke a single lie; in fact, he had not even a single defect in his character. Truthful in speech, honorable in terms of his character, pure in both speech and deed, noble in his manners, easy-going in his

---

[6] Related by Muslim (153), on the authority of Abu Hurayrah.

dealings, good-natured in terms of his disposition, Muhammad the young man was, it is no wonder, universally loved and respected by his fellow tribesmen.

So when he openly announced his prophethood years later, his enemies could not recall a single character flaw, a single slip-up, a single mistake that they could use to attack his character. He had, to their despair and anger, an absolutely clean record. They themselves had labelled him "The Trustworthy One"; they themselves would entrust him and no one else with their valuables; they were the ones who would ask him to settle their disputes. He was, they knew, a paragon of virtues during his youth; imagine, then, how noble and virtuous and good he became once the duties of prophethood fell onto his shoulders.

(سورة القَلَم : ٤) ﴿وَإِنَّكَ لَعَلَىٰ خُلُقٍ عَظِيمٍ ٤﴾

﴿And verily, you [O Muhammad] are on an exalted standard of character.﴾ *(Qur'an 68: 4)*

Muhammad the Messenger

It was, to say the least, tremendous news, amazing news, and life-changing news for everyone on earth: The Seal of all Prophets (ﷺ), after a long wait, had finally come to preach his message to mankind.

﴿۞ عَمَّ يَتَسَآءَلُونَ ١ عَنِ النَّبَإِ ٱلْعَظِيمِ ٢ ٱلَّذِى هُمْ فِيهِ مُخْتَلِفُونَ ٣﴾

(سورة النَّبَإِ : ١-٣)

❨What are they asking [one another]? About the great news, [i.e., Islamic Monotheism, the Qur'an, which Prophet Muhammad brought and the Day of Resurrection, etc.], about which they are in disagreement.❩ *(Qur'an 78: 1-3)*

Kings and peoples of foreign lands, nomads, inhabitants of the Arabian Peninsula — everyone was discussing the Prophet (ﷺ) and his message. It was as if history temporarily stopped while all people took a collective long, deep breath, so that they could absorb the significance of the Prophet's arrival on earth. The earth was spiritually barren and dry, given that the last Prophet before Muhammad (ﷺ) was sent by Allah more than six hundred years earlier, that the message of that previous Prophet — 'Eesa (ﷺ) — was all but lost, and that very few Monotheists remained on earth. If people starve to death in the absence of food and drink, then the inhabitants of the earth, prior to the advent of the Prophet (ﷺ), were spiritually starved, with no nourishment — knowledge and guidance — to keep their souls alive. Therefore, the arrival of the Prophet (ﷺ) on earth was very similar to the falling of rain in a time of drought. In short, the Prophet's arrival represented light: And can light be hidden or shut out?

﴿يُرِيدُونَ لِيُطْفِئُوا نُورَ ٱللَّهِ بِأَفْوَٰهِهِمْ وَٱللَّهُ مُتِمُّ نُورِهِ وَلَوْ كَرِهَ ٱلْكَٰفِرُونَ ۞﴾

(سورة الصَّف : ٨)

❨They intend to put out the Light of Allah [i.e., the Religion of Islam, this Qur'an, and the Prophet Mohammed] with their mouths. But Allah will complete His Light even though the disbelievers hate [it].❩ *(Qur'an 61: 8)*

In fact, it is authentically established that the Messenger of Allah (ﷺ) said: "The example of what Allah sent me with, in terms of guidance and knowledge, is the example of (beneficial) rain (that falls from the sky and causes crops to grow)."[7]

The Prophet (ﷺ) was therefore sent for one main reason: So that Allah alone could be worshipped, without any partners being associated with Him. He was sent so that it could be said on earth, "None has the right to be worshipped but Allah, and Muhammad is the Messenger of Allah". He was sent to uphold the truth, and to crush falsehood. He was sent with clear proofs; with a wonderful and perfect Religion; with justice and kindness; with peace and love; with safety and Faith; with purity, Prayer, charity, fasting, Hajj, and Jihad; with the concepts of enjoining good and forbidding evil; with noble deeds and good manners; and with uprightness and happiness. He was sent to disprove all forms of polytheism, to destroy all false idols, to eradicate ignorance, to wage war against falsehood and oppression, and to deter people from all base and vile manners. Anything that is good, he guided people to it; and anything that is evil, he warned people against it.

When it came to manners, the Prophet (ﷺ) was superior to all other people. And why would he not be so, for it was Allah (ﷻ) who guided him, trained him, and refined his character. As such, the Prophet (ﷺ) had the best manners; he was the most truthful human being in speech; he was the most rightly-guided person; he feared Allah the most; he was the kindest of all people towards his relatives; he was the bravest person to have ever walked the earth; he was the most generous of people; he was the most just of all people; and he was, in every other way, the most superior of all people. All of this was a natural consequence of the

---

[7] Related by Bukhari (79) and Muslim (2282), on the authority of Abu Moosa al-Ash'ari.

Prophet (ﷺ) being nurtured, cared for, trained, and taught by Allah.

Because of his wonderful qualities, the Prophet (ﷺ) was near and dear to the hearts and souls of people. He was blessed and easy-going, and yet he had about himself an aura of dignity and gravity that suited his lofty character. His face shone with the light of guidance; his mouth smiled with love; his heart was truly alive; and his mind was illuminated with elevated thoughts.

He had the uncanny ability of making all those around him happy, and of making all of his Companions feel at ease. While he loved favorable signs (signs that make one feel that something good will happen), he detested evil omens: The former, he (ﷺ) knew, prompted one to be positive and to act well; the latter, on the other hand, made one pessimistic and deterred one from performing good deeds.

It was the Prophet's wont to pardon and forgive the mistakes of others. And he was generous, more generous, in fact, than gentle wind or much-needed rain. He subdued people, not with a sword, but with generosity and good manners. With his message, he brought happiness to mankind. Whoever saw him, loved him; whoever knew him, stood in awe of him; and whoever met him, venerated him. His speech captivated people's hearts, and his noble manners at once tamed and subjugated people's souls.

Allah (ﷻ) made his heart firm and steadfast, so that it never deviated from the truth. Allah guided his speech, so that he (ﷺ) never spoke ignorantly. Allah safeguarded his Faith, so that he never went astray. And Allah supported his mission, so that he was never forsaken or forced into despair. In every way imaginable, he was blessed and guided.

$$\langle \text{﴿وَإِنَّكَ لَعَلَىٰ خُلُقٍ عَظِيمٍ ۝﴾} \rangle \qquad (٤ : سورة القَلَم)$$

﴿And verily, you [O Muhammad] are on an exalted standard of character.﴾

(Qur'an 68: 4)

$$\text{﴿... فَبِمَا رَحْمَةٍ مِنَ اللَّهِ لِنتَ لَهُمْ ۝﴾} \qquad (١٥٩ : سورة آل عِمرَان)$$

﴿And by the Mercy of Allah, you dealt with them gently...﴾

(Qur'an 3: 159)

The Prophet (ﷺ) said: "The person among you who fears Allah the most and is most knowledgeable about Allah, is me."[8] In another hadith, he said: "The best among you is he who is the best towards his family. And among you all, I am the one person who stands out as being the best towards his family."[9] He (ﷺ) is also related to have said: "Verily, I have been sent only to make complete (both in myself and in others) the noblest of manners."[10]

All the Glory be to Allah, Who chose the Prophet (ﷺ), raised him, protected him, guided him, and looked after him.

His religion

His religion is Islam, the only Religion that leads to success and safety. Allah (ﷻ) said:

---

[8] Related by Bukhari (20), on the authority of 'Â'ishah.

[9] Related by Tirmidhi (3895) and by Bayhaqi in *as-Sunan* (15477), on the authority of 'Â'ishah. Tirmidhi said, "This hadith is *ḥasan, Ghareeb* and *ṣaheeh*."

[10] Related by Bayhaqi in *as-Sunan al-Kubrâ* (20571), and by al-Quḍâ'ee in *Musnad ash-Shihâb* (1165). Refer to *Kash al-Khifâ* (638).

﴿وَمَن يَبْتَغِ غَيْرَ ٱلْإِسْلَٰمِ دِينًا فَلَن يُقْبَلَ مِنْهُ وَهُوَ فِى ٱلْءَاخِرَةِ مِنَ ٱلْخَٰسِرِينَ ﴿٨٥﴾﴾

(سورة آل عِمْرَان: ٨٥)

﴾And whoever seeks a religion other than Islam, it will never be accepted of him, and in the Hereafter he will be one of the losers.﴿

(Qur'an 3: 85)

It is the Religion that came to free human beings from the shackles of misguidance; it is an easy Religion; and it is a comprehensive, complete, and perfect Religion.

﴿ ... ٱلْيَوْمَ أَكْمَلْتُ لَكُمْ دِينَكُمْ وَأَتْمَمْتُ عَلَيْكُمْ نِعْمَتِى وَرَضِيتُ لَكُمُ ٱلْإِسْلَٰمَ دِينًا ... ﴿٣﴾﴾

(سورة المَائدة: ٣)

﴾... This day, I have perfected your religion for you, completed My Favor upon you, and have chosen for you Islam as your religion...﴿

(Qur'an 5: 3)

Islam came to free people from servitude to those who themselves are slaves, and to guide them to worship the Lord of all slaves. It came to take them from the narrowness of this world to the vastness of the Hereafter; from the darkness of polytheism to the light of (Islamic) Monotheism; from the misery of disbelief to the happiness of *Eemân* (Faith).

It is a Religion that is at once appropriate and valid for all times and all places. The One Who legislated Islam as a Religion is alone able to forgive sins, and He (ﷻ) alone knows both what His slaves outwardly display and what is hidden in the deepest recesses of their hearts.

This perfect and well-balanced Religion came with beneficial knowledge and good deeds, which is what makes its adherents distinct from Jews and Christians. Jews had knowledge, but it did not benefit them since they did not apply it. Christians, on the other hand, strove to perform good deeds, but since they lacked knowledge, they strayed from the Straight Path. Islam is the Straight Path, the Path that is followed by those who have not incurred upon themselves Allah's wrath, and who are not misguided.

Despite being illiterate, the Messenger of Allah (ﷺ) was sent to recite to people Allah's verses, to purify them, and to teach them the Book and wisdom; for, prior to his advent, they had been in manifest error.

Islam came to forbid lying and the giving of false testimony; it came to forbid oppression and tyranny; it came to forbid cheating people in the buying and selling of goods. Islam came to forbid all forms of wrongdoing. And it also came to preserve the sanctity and dignity of human life — to protect the heart with *Eemân* (Faith); to protect the well-being of the human body, by legislating laws that achieve that effect; to protect people's wealth from being wrongly seized or taken; to protect people's honor from all forms of slander and backbiting; to safeguard people's lives, by forbidding the wrongful shedding of blood; and to protect the mind from anything that diminishes or outright destroys its ability to function properly.

His Book

The Book he was sent with is the Qur'an — categorically the best and the most sacred of all books, the only

Book on the face of the earth that is perfect and that is free from any and all defects. Not a line, not a word, nay, not even a letter of falsehood can be found in any of its pages; which is not surprising, considering that it was revealed by the All-Wise, the One Who is worthy of all praise. Everything about the Qur'an — its meanings, the ordering of its words, the arrangement of its chapters, the legal rulings it contains — is perfect.

What is more, it is a blessed Book: One is blessed when one recites it, when one contemplates its meanings, when one uses it to cure one's physical and spiritual ailments, when people turn to it to judge their disputes, and when one applies its teachings. For each of its letters that one recites, one receives ten rewards.

The Qur'an is the best of companions, being always available, truthful, comforting, trustworthy, and beneficial. It has about it a quality of sweetness. It surpasses all else, but is never surpassed itself. It is neither magic nor poetry nor the speech of man; rather, it is the speech of Allah: From Him it emanated, and to Him it shall return. That most trusted of Angels, Jibreel (عليه السلام), came down with it to the heart of the Messenger of Allah (ﷺ).

The Qur'an was revealed in clear Arabic. To all who know the Arabic language, it is the standard of eloquence, and yet it is a standard that no man can meet or equal or reproduce in any way. It is, moreover, guidance, mercy, an admonition, light, a clear proof, and a cure for what is in the hearts of men. It is divinely protected, so that, no matter how much Islam's enemies try to corrupt or change its verses, it cannot be changed in the least: Allah (عزّ وجلّ) will always protect it from any additions or deletions. As such, the Qur'an is an eternal and lasting miracle.

The Qur'an is a protection for those who follow it; a means of salvation for those who apply its teachings; a gateway towards happiness for those who follow its guidance; and a door to ultimate success for those who turn to it for judgment in every aspect of their lives. The Prophet (ﷺ) said: "Recite the Qur'an; for indeed, it will come as an intercessor for its people (for the people who recite it and apply its teachings) on the Day of Resurrection."[11] According to another narration, the Prophet (ﷺ) said: "The best among you is he who learns the Qur'an and teaches it (to others)."[12] And according to yet another narration, the Prophet (ﷺ) said: "Verily, through this Book, Allah raises certain people; and, through it, He lowers others."[13]

It is the Book that has confuted poets, silenced philosophers, struck dumb the most eloquent of people, amazed scholars, and left speechless the wise.

﴾إِنَّ هَٰذَا ٱلْقُرْءَانَ يَهْدِى لِلَّتِى هِىَ أَقْوَمُ ... ﴿٩﴾﴾ (سورة الإسراء: ٩)

﴾Verily, this Qur'an guides to that which is most just and right...﴿
(Qur'an 17: 9)

Muhammad (ﷺ), the truthful one

Of all men who have ever walked the earth, none has been — nor will any ever be — as truthful as the Prophet (ﷺ). How could anyone come close to him, when he never spoke a single lie in his entire life, not even one that was meant as a joke?

---

[11] Related by Muslim (804), on the authority of Abu Umâmah al-Bâhili.
[12] Related by Bukhari (5027), on the authority of 'Uthmân.
[13] Related by Muslim (817), on the authority of 'Umar.

And while he held himself to a high standard of truthfulness, he ordered his followers to do the same. He said: "Verily, truthfulness leads to *al-Birr* (righteousness, piety), and *al-Birr* leads to Paradise. And a man continues to be truthful and to search out for the truth until, with Allah, he is written as a truthful person..."[14]

The Prophet (ﷺ) informed Muslims that, while a believer might be miserly or cowardly on occasion, he will never lie; furthermore, he forbade Muslims from lying even if they do so only as a joke, in order to make others laugh.

Enough of a testament to his truthfulness is the fact that Allah (ﷻ) entrusted him with the job of conveying His message to both mankind and jinns. The Prophet (ﷺ) then carried out that job with complete truthfulness and trustworthiness, accurately conveying the entire message he was entrusted with, without adding or removing even a single letter of that message.

The Prophet (ﷺ) was truthful on all occasions and in all situations — in times of war and times of peace; when he was happy and when he was angry; when he was serious and when he was joking; when he was engaged in normal conversation and when he issued legal rulings. And he was truthful with all people — with close acquaintances and strangers, with men and women, with friends and enemies. When buying and selling, when signing contracts or treaties, when delivering sermons or writing letters, when issuing legal rulings or telling stories — in these and all other situations, the Prophet (ﷺ) was completely truthful. In fact, he couldn't lie, for Allah not only forbade him from lying, but also protected him from it.

---

[14] Related by Bukhari (6094) and Muslim (2607), on the authority of 'Abdullâh ibn Mas'ood.

The Prophet (ﷺ) was truthful not only in speech, but also with his gestures and signals. For instance, in certain situations, he considered the act of winking to be a lie, because it gave key information to some people, while leaving others in the dark. I am referring here to an incident that actually occurred during the Prophet's lifetime. During the conquest of Makkah, the Prophet (ﷺ) issued a universal pardon to his enemies, with the exception of a few men, men who had especially been cruel, evil, and brutal in the enmity they showed towards Muslims. Such men, the Prophet (ﷺ) announced, were to be killed, even if they were found clutching the covering of the Ka'bah. One of those men was 'Abdullâh ibn Sa'd ibn Abi as-Sarḥ.

'Abdullâh ibn Sa'd knew he was a wanted man, so he went into hiding; he appealed to 'Uthmân ibn 'Affân (﵁) for help. Agreeing to help him, 'Uthmân took him to the Prophet (ﷺ), made him stand before the Prophet (ﷺ) while others were pledging allegiance to him, and said, "O Messenger of Allah, accept the pledge of 'Abdullâh." 'Abdullâh offered his hand three times in order to pledge allegiance, and each time, the Prophet (ﷺ) held back his hand and instead simply fixed his gaze on 'Abdullâh. On 'Abdullâh's fourth try, the Prophet (ﷺ) finally extended his hand, thus accepting 'Abdullâh's pledge to follow and obey him. The Prophet (ﷺ) then went to his Companions and said, "Was there not a sensible man among you who, upon seeing me restrain my hand from accepting his pledge, could have killed him." They replied, "We did not know what you were thinking (when you held your hand back), O Messenger of Allah. Should you not have signalled to us (by winking your eye and by thus informing us that we should kill him)?" The Prophet (Blessings and peace be upon him) replied, "It is not befitting for a Prophet to have a treacherous eye (i.e., it is for this reason that I did not wink to you as a signal)."[15]

Allah (ﷻ) said:

$$﴿ لَيَسْـَٔلَ ٱلصَّـٰدِقِينَ عَن صِدْقِهِمْ ۚ ... ﴾ ٨ ﴾$$

(سورة الأحزاب : ٨)

◖That He may ask the truthful ones [Allah's Messengers and His Prophets] about their truth [i.e., the conveyance of Allah's Message that which they were charged with]...◗   *(Qur'an 33: 8)*

He (ﷻ) also said:

$$﴿ يَـٰٓأَيُّهَا ٱلَّذِينَ ءَامَنُوا۟ ٱتَّقُوا۟ ٱللَّهَ وَكُونُوا۟ مَعَ ٱلصَّـٰدِقِينَ ﴾ ١١٩ ﴾$$

(سورة التوبة : ١١٩)

◖O you who believe! Be afraid of Allah, and be with those who are true [in words and deeds].◗   *(Qur'an 9: 119)*

And in another verse, He (ﷻ) said:

$$﴿ ... فَلَوْ صَدَقُوا۟ ٱللَّهَ لَكَانَ خَيْرًا لَّهُمْ ﴾ ٢١ ﴾$$

(سورة محمّد : ٢١)

◖... Then if they had been true to Allah, it would have been better for them.◗   *(Qur'an 47: 21)*

The Prophet (ﷺ) was truthful with Allah, truthful with himself, truthful with his family, truthful with his friends, truthful with people in general, and even truthful with his enemies. Had the truth been an actual man, that man would have been Muhammad (ﷺ). He was known as, "The Truthful, Trustworthy One" prior to the advent of Islam; imagine, then, how he became

---

[15] Related by Abu Dâwood (4359) and Nasâ'i (4067).

once he began to receive revelation from his Lord (ﷻ), once he became a Prophet, once he became blessed with guidance and uprightness.

Muhammad, the patient one

*I*n the English language, patience is sometimes defined as the capacity for calm endurance of pain, trouble, and inconvenience. As an Islamic virtue, patience has an additional spiritual quality to it: To endure hardships for the sake of Allah, consciously making the intention that, by being patient and by not complaining, one will hopefully receive rewards from Allah (ﷻ) in the Hereafter. After all, many hardy people in this world calmly endure pain and hardship; but relatively few people do so for the sake of Allah.

As for the Prophet (ﷺ), he was a paragon of patience. For him, being chosen to be the seal of Prophets meant, not an easy life, but a life of difficulties and hardships, of trials and tribulations, of pain and suffering. In fact, no one in the history of mankind faced as many hardships as did the Prophet (ﷺ). Death would have been easier than the personal tragedies the Prophet (ﷺ) experienced throughout his life, and yet he never complained, but instead remained steadfast, patient, and thankful to his Lord. In being patient, he was obeying his Lord's command:

(سورة النّحل: ١٢٧) ﴾... وَٱصْبِرْ وَمَا صَبْرُكَ إِلَّا بِٱللَّهِ ۝﴿

﴾And endure you patiently [O Muhammad], your patience is not but from Allah...﴿ *(Qur'an 16: 127)*

He (ﷺ) patiently endured being an orphan, being poor, and being hungry. He was patient when he was forced to leave his homeland, his house, and his family. He was patient when he was being persecuted, when some of his Companions were being tortured, and when others among his family members and Companions were killed. He was patient when his enemies waged war against him, when Bedouins acted ignorantly with him, when Jews plotted against him, when hypocrites conspired to harm him, when many of his own relatives forsook him and declared war upon him.

He was patient in other ways as well. He patiently resisted the temptations of this world, the allure of riches, and the appeal of being strong and powerful. He turned away from all of the above because, instead of those worldly attractions, he longed only to please his Lord.

In every aspect of his life, and in every stage of his prophethood, the Prophet (ﷺ) was patient. Patience, in fact, was his armor against everything that is harmful in this life. Every time he remembered what his enemies said, he recalled the words of Allah (ﷻ):

(سورة طه : ١٣٠) ﴿فَٱصْبِرْ عَلَىٰ مَا يَقُولُونَ ... ﴿١٣٠﴾﴾

❴So bear patiently [O Muhammad] what they say...❵

(Qur'an 20: 130)

Every time a difficult situation became almost too difficult to bear, he remembered the saying of Allah (ﷻ):

(سورة يُوسُف : ١٨) ﴿ ... فَصَبْرٌ جَمِيلٌ ... ﴿١٨﴾﴾

❴... So [for me] patience is most fitting...❵   *(Qur'an 12: 18)*

And every time he faced almost certain destruction at the hands of his enemies, he remembered Allah's saying:

$$﴿فَٱصۡبِرۡ كَمَا صَبَرَ أُو۟لُوا۟ ٱلۡعَزۡمِ مِنَ ٱلرُّسُلِ ... ﴿٣٥﴾﴾$$ (سورة الأحقاف : ٣٥)

❝Therefore be patient [O Muhammad] as did the Messengers of strong will...❞ *(Qur'an 46: 35)*

His was the patience of a man who is perfectly confident that Allah (ﷻ) will help him and that Allah will reward him for his travails and for his patience. His was the patience of a man who knew that Allah was with him and that Allah was all the help he needed in life. As such, nothing — no harsh word, no curse, no rude behavior, and no physical torture — could shake him, faze him, perturb him, or even annoy him.

When his uncle died, he was patient. When his wife died, he was patient. When Ḥamzah (ﷺ) died, he was patient, even though Ḥamzah was killed in an especially gruesome manner. When he was forced to leave Makkah, he was patient. When his son died, he was patient. When most of his people rejected his message, he remained patient. When his pure and chaste wife was accused of doing a vile deed, he remained patient, seeking help from none save Allah. When his people labelled him a poet, a sorcerer, a madman, and a liar, he remained patient. When they cursed him, persecuted him, waged war against him, and physically assaulted him, he remained patient. In short, he was, and continues to remain, the Imam (leader) of those who practice patience, and the ideal role model of those who are thankful.

Muhammad, the generous one

Of all of Allah's created beings, none has ever been as generous as the Prophet (ﷺ). There are reasons why he was so generous: He was sent to adorn himself and others with the noblest of manners; when he gave others, he expected nothing in return from them, desiring instead to be rewarded by Allah alone; and, perhaps most importantly, he trusted in Allah so much that he did not fear poverty.

Because the Prophet (ﷺ) possessed the above-mentioned qualities, he became the very personification of generosity. An Arab poet once noted that the Prophet (ﷺ) would have altogether forsaken the word 'no', had it not been for *Tashahud* (the testimony of Faith):

He said 'no' never, except when he made Tashahud,
Had it not been for the Tashahud, his 'no'
would have been a 'yes'.

What the poet meant, of course, is that, whenever someone went to the Prophet (ﷺ) and asked him for something — money, food, clothing, or something else — he (ﷺ) would never say, 'No'. But he did use the word 'no' in the Testimony of Faith: "No one has the right to be worshipped but Allah."

Among Arabs, certain historical figures are still remembered for their generosity — the likes of Haram, Ibn Jad'ân, and perhaps most famously, Hâtim. And yet none of these men even approached the generosity of the Prophet (ﷺ). Without thinking twice about the matter, the Prophet (ﷺ) once gave a man an entire flock of sheep that were so numerous that they filled the valley that separated two mountains. At around the same time, he gave each chieftain of various Arab tribes one hundered camels. On one occasion, a man asked the Prophet (ﷺ) for the very shirt he had on his back; in response to the man's strange request, the Prophet (ﷺ) removed his shirt and handed it over to the man.

When the Prophet (ﷺ) showed generosity, he expected nothing in return. Many rich men, especially kings, give charity, hoping not for a monetary return, but instead for respect, love, admiration, loyalty, or maybe even just an obsequious kiss on the hand. The Prophet (ﷺ) expected none of these things; nay, he acted so humbly that he made a person feel that, by taking something from the Prophet (ﷺ), he was the one who was doing the Prophet (ﷺ) a favour, and not vice-versa. Or in the words of a poet,

You see him, when you go to him, with a cheerful expression on his face,
Making it seem that you are the one giving him that which you ask for.

If the Prophet (ﷺ) had nothing when someone asked him for something, he would find something to give him. And when he had very little himself, he would give away what little he had, trusting that Allah would reward him and provide for him.

When the spoils of war would be gathered, he would distribute them in less than an hour. His table-spread was like a complementary food stand — any and all comers were welcome to it, except that they were welcome to take generous portions. His home was the Makkah of all travellers and strangers.

Everyone benefited from the Prophet's generosity: The traveller he treated as a guest; the hungry he provided with food; his relatives he honored with good treatment; to the needy he gave without fear of poverty; the rich and the poor alike he treated well; Jews, Bedouins, enemies, and hypocrites all ate with him as his guests. It is not mentioned in any narration that the Prophet (ﷺ) ever became weary of being generous, ever said 'no' to someone who asked him for help, or ever showed the least bit of displeasure towards someone who demanded his assistance. On one occasion, a Bedouin pulled back violently at the collar of the Prophet's robe, so violently, in fact, that a mark was left on the Prophet's neck. The Bedouin then said, "Give me from what you have in terms of Allah's wealth; from the wealth that is neither your father's nor your mother's." The Prophet (ﷺ) turned to the Bedouin, laughed good-naturedly, and then gave him a generous share of wealth.

When a treasure of gold or silver would come to him, he would distribute it immediately, without saving even a coin from it for himself. When he gave someone money, he was happier to give than was the other person to receive.

A paragon of generosity himself, the Prophet (ﷺ) exhorted Muslims to follow his example. He said: "Whoever believes in Allah and the Last Day, let him be generous to his guest."[16] In another narration, he said: "Every person will be under the shade of his own charity (on the Day of Resurrection), until judgment is rendered among people."[17] According to yet another narration, he

---

[16] Related by Bukhari (6018, 6136, 6138) and Muslim (47), on the authority of Abu Hurayrah.

[17] On the authority of 'Uqbah ibn 'Âmir, this hadith is related by Ibn Khuzaymah in his Ṣaḥeeḥ (2431); by Ibn Ḥibbân in his Ṣaḥeeḥ (3310) and by Abu Na'eem in al-Ḥilyah (8/181).

said: "Charity never causes one's level of wealth to decrease."[18] To give is to be blessed: Whatever you give away in charity, you get back in some form or another.

Prophet Muhammad's bravery

$\mathcal{B}$y now, the reader should know that all of the Prophet's noble characteristics were direct results of certain causes — such as his strong Faith in Allah, his fear of Allah, and the complete trust he (ﷺ) placed in Allah (ﷻ). In this regard, the characteristic of bravery is no exception. The Prophet (ﷺ) was a paragon of bravery because he feared no one save Allah, because he had Faith in Allah's Promise to protect him from his enemies, and because he placed his complete trust in Allah.

As such, he was like a great mountain, in that he did not easily shake or tremble, but instead remained firm and steadfast through the most harrowing of situations. His enemy's threats did not perturb him; life-threatening situations did not frighten him; and the threat of physical harm or even of death did not faze him in the least.

He placed his complete trust in Allah, seeking no one's help save His help, being confident in His Promise, and being satisfied and happy with His decree. With such wonderful qualities, it is not surprising that he personally fought in battles, placing himself in harm's way even when few, if any, others were willing to do the same.

---

[18] Related by Muslim (2588), on the authority of Abu Hurayrah.

Never once did the Prophet (ﷺ) flee from a battle; never once did he even retreat a single step when fighting intensified. In fact, when heads were decapitated; when swords sliced through air, skin, flesh, and bones; when many people met their deaths in a matter of minutes or seconds; when swords clashed with shields, and when arrows penetrated armor — the Prophet (ﷺ) was the closest member of his army to the enemy. At times, Companions used the Prophet (ﷺ) as a shield, knowing that they would stand a better chance against their enemy if they rallied around the Prophet (ﷺ).

For the Prophet (ﷺ), it did not matter how many enemy soldiers there were on a battlefield; it did not matter how many weapons they had; these things did not matter because he believed with certainty that, regardless of the strength of the enemy, Allah would help him overcome them. On the Day of Hunayn, most Muslims fled from the battlefield during the initial stages of the battle. The only Muslims who remained steadfast on the battlefield were the Prophet (ﷺ) and six of his Companions; and this verse was revealed to him:

$$﴾فَقَاتِلْ فِي سَبِيلِ ٱللَّهِ لَا تُكَلَّفُ إِلَّا نَفْسَكَ وَحَرِّضِ ٱلْمُؤْمِنِينَ ... ﴿٨٤﴾﴾$$

(سورة النِّسَاء: ٨٤)

﴾Then fight [O Muhammad] in the Cause of Allah, you are not tasked [i.e., held responsible] except for yourself, and incite the believers [to fight along with you]...﴿ *(Qur'an 4: 84)*

The Prophet (ﷺ) was neither nervous nor frightened during times of battle; instead, he was calm and at peace, for he desired martyrdom at least as much as he desired victory.

As a result of the Prophet's bravery, he sometimes sustained injuries — for instance, during the Battle of Badr, he fractured a bone in his face, and one of his front teeth broke. In a single battle, he lost seventy of his Companions . And yet he never became weak, cowardly, or fearful; instead, he ploughed forward on the battlefield as if he wanted to die.

On the Day of Badr, he not only led his army, but also took part in the fighting during the most intense and dangerous stages of the battle. During the Battle of Khandaq, the Confederate armies were apparently in complete control of the situation, confident that it was only a matter of time before they broke the siege and destroyed the Muslims of Madeenah. As for Muslim soldiers, their hearts reached their throats, so afraid were they; they were shaken and put to trial, with at least some of them being on the verge of hopelessness; meanwhile, the Prophet (ﷺ) remained patient, steadfast, and confident of victory. But as confident as he was, he did not forget to invoke Allah for help. He stood up, prayed, supplicated, and invoked his Lord for help, until Allah answered his Prayers and caused his enemies to be defeated, to suffer humiliation, and to retreat in disgrace even though they greatly outnumbered their Muslim counterparts. The violent wind that Allah (ﷻ) sent to the Confederate armies instilled terror into the hearts of polytheist soldiers, and thus the siege came to an end. And on the night of Badr, the Muslims fell asleep; as for the Prophet (ﷺ), he stood up, prayed, and invoked Allah for help.

No one was as brave as was the Prophet (ﷺ), who said: "By the One Who has my soul in His Hand, I would love to be killed in the way of Allah, to then be resurrected, and to then be killed (again)."[19]

---

[19] Related by Bukhari (36, 2797) and Muslim (1876), on the authority of Abu Hurayrah.

The Prophet's Zuhd

*Z*uhd is an often misunderstood term, most probably because, among certain people — namely, certain followers of Sufi orders — it is taken to an extreme; or, it is understood only on a superficial level. In the Arabic language, a *Zâhid* — one who practices *Zuhd* — is someone who is abstemious, austere, and self-denying in his lifestyle. As an Islamic term, a *Zâhid* is someone who abjures worldly pleasures and comforts for the sake of Allah, and because, through leading a self-denying existence in this life, he hopes to enjoy a comfortable and pleasure-filled life in the Hereafter.

Suffice it to say, the Prophet (ﷺ) was the Imam (leader) of all *Zâhids*. His *Zuhd* was based on his certain knowledge that this world is a fleeting abode: Its pleasures are few, limited, and temporary; and life passes by so quickly that all people who live to be old agree that their lives went by quickly, that it seemed only yesterday that they were children. Such a life, therefore, cannot be compared to the everlasting life of the Hereafter.

The Prophet (ﷺ) kept his sight focused on the Hereafter, being very cognizant of what Allah (ﷻ) has prepared for His believing slaves in terms of rewards, comfort, pleasures, and eternal bliss. As such, he refused to take from this world anything that was above and beyond his basic needs. He understood that, the more one possesses in this life, the more attached one becomes to this world.

The Prophet (ﷺ) was a *Zâhid* not by force of circumstances, but by choice. As the leader of a Nation, but moreover as a favored and beloved Prophet of Allah, he could have had mountains of gold and silver; he could have led a luxurious and comfortable lifestyle: He only had to ask Allah, and he would have been given great wealth. But he preferred to follow the way of *Zuhd*, to save his share of good things for the Hereafter. As a result of that choice, he spent many nights of his life hungry; at times, at least a month would pass by without a cooking fire being ignited in his house. During such periods of hardships, he would either go hungry for days, or he and his family would survive on water and dates. As one of his wives stated, it never occurred that he ate a satisfying amount of barley bread for three consecutive nights. He would sleep not on a real mattress, but on a makeshift bed that was made of straw, one that would leave marks on the side of his body. On various occasions of his life, he would stave off the pangs of hunger by tying a rock around his stomach. His Companions (may Allah be pleased with them all), who themselves suffered frequently from want, were often saddened to see the signs of hunger on the Prophet's face.

As for the Prophet's house, it was made neither of bricks nor cement nor any other strong, resistant, and long-lasting material; it was, on the contrary, made of simple clay. It was small, and its roof was low. And rather than depend on the help of his Companions, the Prophet (ﷺ) once left his armor as collateral with a Jew, so that he could borrow from him thirty *Ṣā's* of dates (a single *Ṣā'* is equal to four handfuls of something). His clothing was simple and plain, and never once did he sit at a dining table to eat. He underwent such hardships in order to discipline his soul, to preserve his Faith, and to be deserving of the promise that Allah (ﷻ) made to him:

﴿وَلَسَوْفَ يُعْطِيكَ رَبُّكَ فَتَرْضَىٰ ۞﴾

(سورة الضحىٰ: ٥)

❨And verily, your Lord will give you [all, i.e., good] so that you shall be well-pleased.❩ *(Qur'an 93: 5)*

Upon receiving wealth (such as certain kinds of war booty), the Prophet (ﷺ) would distribute it among the people, without keeping a single dirham for himself. If he hoped that certain people would embrace Islam, he would, in order to encourage them, give them all of the camels, cows, and sheep he had in his possession. And he would then walk away without keeping a single camel, cow, or sheep for himself. He once said: "If I had wealth that was equal in quantity to the trees of *Tihâmah* (i.e., a very large sum of wealth), I would have distributed it, and you would not have found me to be a miser, a liar, or a coward (regarding the manner in which I would liberally give away all of that wealth)."[20]

In the way he (ﷺ) turned away from this world, without rejoicing in its treasures or enjoying its pleasures; and in the way he focused on the Hereafter, performing deeds purely for the sake of Allah — the Prophet (ﷺ) became the ideal role model for all *Zâhids*, and, more generally, for all Muslims. Even though he had the wealth of a Nation at his disposal, and even though his Companions would have given him all of their wealth if he had only asked, he built no castle, and saved no money. When he died, he left hardly any material possessions behind. And whatever he did leave behind was earmarked for charity, for he said: "We (we group of Prophets) are not inherited from; whatever we leave behind is charity."[21]

---

[20] Related by Mâlik, in *al-Muwaṭṭa* (977); and by aṭ-Ṭabarâni, in *al-Awsaṭ* (1864). Refer also to *al-Kâmil*, by Ibn 'Adi (3/97).

[21] Related by Bukhari (3093, 3712) and Muslim (1758).

I do not say for nothing that the Prophet (ﷺ) could have been rich if he only wanted to be, for Allah did in fact give him a choice between being a king/Messenger and a slave (of Allah)/Messenger. The Prophet (ﷺ) chose the latter option, and so he ate his fill one day, and he went hungry the very next day, a process that more or less continued until he met his Lord.

Since the Prophet (ﷺ) cared so little about this world, he did not ever think twice about giving away his wealth to others, which was another reason why he was so generous. He never said 'no' to someone who asked him for help, and he never disappointed the hopes of someone who expected something from him. He (ﷺ) said: "If, for Allah, this world was worth even the wing of a mosquito, He would not have given a disbeliever in it even a mouthful of water."[22] According to another narration, he said, "Live in this world as if you are a stranger or a traveller who is only passing through (one place on his way to a distant destination)."

It is related that he said: "Seek little from this world, and Allah will love you; refrain from taking what people have (with them), and people will love you."[23] He (ﷺ) also said: "What do I have to do with this world! Verily, the example of me vis-à-vis this world is nothing more than the example of a man who takes a noon-time nap underneath the shade of a tree, and who then gets up and leaves it."[24]

---

[22] Tirmidhi (2320).

[23] Related by Ibn Mâjah (4102); by aṭ-Ṭabarâni, in *al-Kabeer* (10522); by al-Ḥâkim (7833), on the authority of Sahl ibn Saʻd as-Sâʻidi. Refer to *as-Silsilat al-Aḥâdeeth aṣ-Ṣaheeḥah* (944).

[24] Related by Aḥmad (3701, 4196), Tirmidhi (2377) and Ibn Mâjah (4109), on the authority of ʻAbdullâh ibn Masʻood. Tirmidhi said, "This hadith is *ḥasan ṣaheeḥ*."

The Prophet (ﷺ) also said: "The world is cursed, and everything in it is cursed — except for the remembrance of Allah, for good deeds that Allah loves, for a scholar, or for a student."[25] And according to yet another hadith, he (ﷺ) said: "All that you have from your wealth is what you eat and thus cause to be used up; what you wear and thus cause to be worn out; and what you give in charity and thus cause to remain (for your benefit)."[26]

Prophet Muhammad's humbleness

To be humble is to be modest, self-effacing, unpretentious, and unostentatious; it involves showing a low estimation of one's own importance. It is the opposite of being arrogant, proud, and haughty.

Many people are humble for various reasons — because they truly suffer from low self-esteem, because they want to put on an air of piety, or because they genuinely want to be good people. The Prophet's humbleness was the humbleness of a man who knew the greatness and mightiness of his Lord; of one who was shy of his Lord; of one who glorified Allah in a manner that is befitting of His Majesty. Thus knowing that Allah is the Greatest and that He is All-Powerful, the Prophet (ﷺ) understood that it was sheer folly to be proud or to put on airs of superiority. No matter how proud some people were of their status, no matter how much wealth rich people owned, no matter how arrogant kings

---

[25] Related by Tirmidhi (2322) and Ibn Mâjah (4112), on the authority of Abu Hurayrah.

[26] Related by Muslim (2958).

became because of their power — in reality they were all weak and insignificant, they were all petty creatures, and they were all poor and needy to Allah. How could the Prophet (ﷺ) be in awe of titles, status, pride, power, and wealth when he travelled with his soul to Allah and knew the reality of this life compared to the Hereafter? As a result of his strong Faith in Allah, the Prophet (ﷺ) ceased to be impressed by the things that other human beings became impressed with. He became a true slave of his Lord, and he became humble towards believers.

The Prophet (ﷺ) would stand beside an elderly woman and help her; he would visit sick people; he would show mercy and compassion to the poor; he paid attention to the needs of the miserable and the forlorn; he consoled the weak; he played with children; he joked with his family; he was easy-going and easily accessible to others; he sat on dirt and slept on the ground; sand would be his bed, and straw would be his pillow. He was pleased with what Allah decreed for him. Status, fame, power, material possessions — none of these things mattered to him.

It is often said that you can know the character of a person based on how he treats those below him, those who are deemed weak in society. As for the Prophet (ﷺ), he was the best friend and greatest supporter of the weak. He spoke gently to women, using kind words; he helped the poor and needy; and he addressed strangers with a tone of love and compassion.

The Prophet (ﷺ) would always smile when looking at the faces of his Companions, and he would say: "Verily, I am nothing more than a slave (of Allah); as such, I eat as a slave eats, and I sit down as a slave sits down."[27]

---

[27] Related by Ibn Abu 'Āṣim, in *az-Zuhd* (1/6); and by Ibn Sa'd, in *aṭ-=*

On one occasion, a man went to the Prophet (ﷺ), and was so much in awe of him that his body began to tremble. Seeing the man's condition, the Prophet (ﷺ) said: "Take it easy on yourself! For indeed, I am the son of a woman who would eat *al-Qadeed* (salted meat that was first dried in the sun, i.e., she would eat simple food) in Makkah."[28]

The Prophet (ﷺ) disliked being praised. He said to his Companions: "Do not praise me in the same way that the Christians praised 'Eesa ibn Maryam. For indeed, I am nothing more than the slave of Allah and His Messenger; therefore, say (i.e., call me) the slave of Allah and His Messenger."[29] The Prophet (ﷺ) would forbid people from standing up to meet him or from standing above his head (as a means of honoring him). If he arrived at a gathering, he would not ask someone to move, so that he could sit in a prominent position in the gathering; instead, he would simply sit where there was space, which usually meant beside the person who had arrived just before he did.

Rather than sit in exclusive gatherings, the Prophet (ﷺ) would intermingle among the general population of Muslims, as if he were one of them — of the same rank and status. And he would accept other people's invitations; he would say: "If I were to be invited to a meal that consisted only of the foot (of a sheep), I would accept the invitation; and if I were to be given an arm (of a sheep) as a gift, I would accept it."[30]

= *Ṭabaqât* (1/371). Refer to *Kashf al-Khifâ* (1/17).

[28] Related by Ibn Mâjah (3312) and al-Ḥâkim (4366), on the authority of Abu Mas'ood. Refer to *al-Kâmil*, by Ibn 'Adi (6/286).

[29] Related by Bukhari (3445), on the authority of Ibn 'Abbâs.

[30] Related by Bukhari (2568, 5178).

The Prophet (ﷺ) loved poor people. It is related that he said: "O Allah, keep me alive as a poor person, make me die as a poor person, and resurrect me among the company of poor people."[31] The Prophet (ﷺ) forbade Muslims from adopting the characteristic that is the opposite of humbleness, namely, pride or arrogance; and he despised proud and arrogant people. He said: "On the Day of Resurrection, the arrogant ones will be resurrected as small ants (in size but not in actual appearance); humiliation will cover and envelop them from all directions."[32] To be arrogant means to vie with Allah in greatness, majesty, and glory — qualities that are specific to Allah. In a *Qudsee* hadith, the Prophet (ﷺ) related that Allah said: "Glory is my robe, and greatness is my lower garment. If anyone vies with me in either of these qualities, I will cast him into the Hellfire."[33]

All people felt a great deal of sincere love for the Prophet (ﷺ). And why wouldn't they? After all, he was a sincere friend and helper of the weak and poor. He would, for instance, walk alongside a young servant-girl, going wherever she would take him in order to help her with an errand. And he would visit Umm Aiman (ﵞ), who was a freed slave.

When the 'Âmir ibn Ṣa'ṣa'ah delegation visited him, its members said to the Prophet (ﷺ): "You are the best of us, and the noblest among us. You are our chief, and the son of our chief."

---

[31] Related by Tirmidhi (2352), on the authority of Anas; by Ibn Mâjah (4126) and by al-Ḥâkim (7911), on the authority of Abu Sa'eed al-Khudri. And al-Ḥâkim declared the authenticity of this hadith.

[32] Related by Aḥmad (6639) and Tirmidhi (2492); refer to *Kashf al-Khifâ* (3236).

[33] Related by Muslim (2620) and Abu Dâwood (4090), and the above-mentioned wording is taken from Abu Dâwood's narration of the hadith.

The Prophet (ﷺ) replied, "O people, say what you have come to say, or at least say some of the things you have said (without praising me excessively); and do not allow the Devil (the *Shayṭân*) to make you his helpers and followers."[34] And the Prophet (ﷺ) became angry when a man said to him, "Whatever Allah wills (happens), and whatever you will (happens)." The Prophet (ﷺ) said, "Woe upon you! Have you made me an equal unto Allah! Instead, say, 'Whatever Allah alone wills (happens).'"[35]

What leader can claim to be as humble as the Prophet (ﷺ)? He would run errands for his family; he would mend his own shoes; he would sow patches on his clothing; he would sweep the floor of his home; he would milk his sheep; he would cut meat for his family; he would personally serve food to his guests; he would be kind and generous to his guests, not just with food, but also with his pleasant company; he would take turns riding and walking with his travel companion; he would eat barley; he would sometimes walk barefoot; he would sleep in the Masjid; he would ride behind another rider, so that, while he sat in an uncomfortable position, his riding partner would sit comfortably on a saddle; he would help the poor and weak; and, among a company of travellers, he would linger in the rear of the group, so that he could help those who were weak and who were unable to keep up with the others.

O Allah, send prayers and salutations upon Your Prophet (ﷺ) for as long as tongues utter his name, and for as long as he is spoken about and remembered by both human beings and jinns.

---

[34] Related by Aḥmad (15876) and Abu Dâwood (4806).
[35] Related by Aḥmad (1842, 2557); and by Nasâ'i in *as-Sunan al-Kubrâ* (10825), on the authority of Ibn 'Abbâs.

Prophet Muhammad's forbearance

$\mathcal{T}$o be a forbearing person is to be tolerant, patient, moderate, lenient, and forgiving. According to its dictionary definition, forbearance means, "Abstinence from enforcing what is due..."[36] Therefore, when someone wrongs you, you are forbearing when you abstain 'from enforcing what is due,' when you refrain from exacting revenge.

Without a doubt, the Messenger of Allah (ﷺ) was the most forbearing of people. When personally wronged, he would restrain his anger and forgive the person who wronged him. He would forego his personal rights, but not the rights of Allah (ﷺ). After a group of fellow tribesmen rejected his message, called him a 'liar' and a 'magician,' persecuted him for a number of years, forced him to leave his homeland, and then waged war against him for another long period of time — after all of that, the Prophet (ﷺ) forgave them, saying to them on the day of the Conquest of Makkah: "Go (forth in safety), for you are the freed ones."[37]

Also on the Day of the Conquest of Makkah, the Prophet (ﷺ) forgave his cousin Sufiyân ibn al-Hârith. Sufiyân said to the Prophet (ﷺ) that day: "By Allah, Allah preferred you over us, and we were certainly in the wrong." The Prophet (ﷺ) replied by recited the following verse:

---

[36] Excerpted from *Oxford Talking Dictionary*. Copyright 1998, The Learning Company, Inc. All Rights Reserved.

[37] Related by ash-Shâfi'ee, in *al-Umm* (7/361); by aṭ-Ṭabari, in his *Târeekh* (2/161); and by Bayhaqi, in *as-Sunan al-Kubrâ* (18055). Refer to *Ṣaḥeeh al-Jâmi'* (4815).

﴿ ... لَا تَثْرِيبَ عَلَيْكُمُ ٱلْيَوْمَ يَغْفِرُ ٱللَّهُ لَكُمْ وَهُوَ أَرْحَمُ ٱلرَّٰحِمِينَ ٩٢ ﴾

(سورة يُوسُف : ٩٢)

﴾... No reproach on you this day, may Allah forgive you, and He is the Most Merciful of those who show mercy!﴿ *(Qur'an 12: 92)*

Bedouins were notorious for being rude and inappropriate in their behavior towards the Prophet (ﷺ), and yet the Prophet (ﷺ) reciprocated their harshness not with harshness of his own, but with forbearance and forgiveness, thus obeying the command of his Lord, Who said:

(سورة الحِجر : ٨٥) ﴿ ... فَٱصْفَحِ ٱلصَّفْحَ ٱلْجَمِيلَ ٨٥ ﴾

﴾... So overlook [O Muhammad] their faults with gracious forgiveness.﴿ *(Qur'an 15: 85)*

When one of Allah's laws would be violated, none became angrier than the Prophet (ﷺ). But when the Prophet (ﷺ) would be personally wronged — cursed, verbally abused, etc. — he would restrain his anger, show forgiveness, and abstain from exacting revenge. In fact, when he had cause to be angry, he would become even more forbearing than he normally was, perhaps even smiling at the person who wronged him. And he advised his Companions to also avoid anger, saying to one of them: "Do not be angry. Do not be angry. Do not be angry."[38]

If someone conveyed to him evil words that had been spoken about him, the Prophet (ﷺ) would not investigate the matter, trying to find out who spoke against him. If he knew the identity of the man who spoke against him, he would neither

---

[38] Related by Bukhari (6116).

reproach him nor censure him. And he would even forbid his Companions from informing him about anything negative that someone might have said about him. He said: "Let no one among you convey to me what is said about me (in terms of what will give rise to bad feelings in my heart). For indeed, I love to (leave my home and) come out to you with a pure and clean heart (towards each one of you i.e., I want to come out without having negative feelings about any of you as a result of what I know one of you said about me)."[39]

One day, when 'Abdullâh ibn Mas'ood (﴿﴾) told the Prophet (﴿﴾) what someone said about him, the Prophet (﴿﴾) replied: "May Allah have mercy on Moses: He was harmed even more than this (i.e., even more than I have been harmed), and yet he remained patient."[40]

There are different levels of forgiveness: On the one hand, there is the forgiveness of the weak and meek, those who do not have the means or the ability to exact revenge against the person who wronged them. Then, on the other hand, there is the forgiveness granted by the strong, those who have the means, the ability, and the opportunity to punish the one who wronged them. To be sure, the latter kind of forgiveness is at once superior and uncommon. But it is the very kind of forgiveness that the Prophet (﴿﴾) showed to his enemies. When he conquered Makkah, he had with him thousands of soldiers, each one of whom would have been more than happy to punish the men who disbelieved in, persecuted, and waged war against the Prophet (﴿﴾) for so many

---

[39] Related by Ahmad (3750), Abu Dâwood (4860), and Tirmidhi (3896), on the authority of 'Abdullâh ibn Mas'ood.
[40] Related by Bukhari (3150, 3405) and Muslim (1062).

years. Thus the Prophet (ﷺ) had the means, the ability, and the opportunity to punish his enemies. But he didn't do so, deciding instead to pardon them.

The Prophet (ﷺ) once said: "If one holds back his anger, then Allah will hold back His Punishment from him."[41] On one occasion, when a man said to the Prophet (ﷺ), "Be just," the Prophet (ﷺ) became neither angry nor vindictive; instead, he replied, "I will indeed fail and lose (ultimately in the Hereafter) if I am not just."[42] And when a number of Jews spoke rudely with him, he forgave them. His forbearance had the effect of extinguishing the flames of enmity in the hearts of people.

﴿ٱدْفَعْ بِٱلَّتِي هِيَ أَحْسَنُ ٱلسَّيِّئَةَ نَحْنُ أَعْلَمُ بِمَا يَصِفُونَ ۝﴾

(سورة المؤمنون: ٩٦)

❴Repel evil with that which is better. We are Best-Acquainted with the things they utter.❵ *(Qur'an 23: 96)*

The true test of forbearance comes when one deals with one's family or with those under one's command. When one goes out into the world, it is relatively easy to be forbearing and forgiving. When a person is wronged out in public, one will generally be civil, if not outright forgiving, because one does not want to be regarded in society as being harsh, rude, or vindictive; and because one does not want to get into any trouble. Among one's family, however, one is protected by a screen of privacy, by

---

[41] Related by Abu Ya'la (4338); and by Bayhaqi, in *ash-Shu'ab*. Refer also to *al-'Ilal*, by Ibn Abi Ḥâtim (1919); and to *Majmâ' az-Zawâid* (10/298).

[42] Related by Bukhari (3138) and Muslim (1063). The above-mentioned wording is from the narration of Muslim, who related it on the authority of Jâbir ibn 'Abdullâh.

the walls of one's home. One can be angry without the fear of being judged by society. And when one shows anger at those who are under one's command, one is not fearful of getting arrested or of getting into any other kind of trouble.

As for the Prophet (ﷺ), he was kind and forbearing both towards his family and towards those who were under his command. He joked with his family; he was gentle and kind towards them; and he forgave them their shortcomings. And whenever he was with them, he would both smile and laugh, thus establishing for them a blissful and happy domestic life.

The Prophet (ﷺ) was as forbearing towards those under his command as he was towards others. Anas ibn Mâlik (ﷺ) said: "I served the Messenger of Allah (ﷺ) for ten years; and throughout that entire period, he never once said regarding something I did, 'Why did you do that?' And he never once said regarding something I didn't do, 'Why didn't you do that?'" Everyone who came into contact with the Prophet (ﷺ) was immediately impressed by his smiling countenance, easy-going manner, friendly demeanor, and forgiving nature. Their amazement quickly turned into admiration, and then into love that became firmly rooted in their hearts.

Prophet Muhammad's mercy

Allah (ﷺ) described the Prophet (ﷺ) as follows:

﴿وَمَآ أَرْسَلْنَٰكَ إِلَّا رَحْمَةً لِّلْعَٰلَمِينَ ﴿١٠٧﴾﴾ (سورة الأنبياء: ١٠٧)

❪And We have sent you [O Muhammad] not but as a mercy for the 'Âlameen [mankind, jinns, and all that exists].❫ *(Qur'an 21: 107)*

It is related that the Prophet (Blessings and peace be upon him) said about himself: "Verily, I am nothing more than a mercy and a guide."[43] Once, upon seeing his daughter's son dying, the Prophet (ﷺ) began to cry. When someone asked him about his crying, he said, "Verily, this is mercy which Allah places in the heart of whomsoever He wills from His slaves. And verily, Allah has mercy only on those among his slaves who are themselves merciful."[44]

The Prophet (ﷺ) was equally merciful towards relatives, friends, and strangers; after all, Allah (ﷻ) described him as being a mercy, not just to friends and relatives, not even just to Muslims, but to all that exists.

In everything he did, the Prophet (Blessings and peace be upon him) tried to make matters easy for his people. For instance, when he wanted to prolong the congregational Prayer, and when he would then hear the crying of a baby, he would shorten the length of his Prayer, so as to avoid making matters difficult for the baby's mother. On one occasion, when Umâmah bint Zaynab (may Allah be pleased with her) cried while Muslims were performing congregational Prayer, the Prophet (ﷺ) picked her up and continued to lead the people in Prayer. Then, when he

---

[43] Related by ad-Dârimi (15) in a narration whose chain is *Mursal* (disconnected, in that the name of the Companion who related the hadith is not mentioned); however, al-Ḥakim related the same saying in a narration whose chain is connected. Al-Ḥakim related it on the authority of Abu Hurayrah, and ruled that it is authentic (100).

[44] Related by Bukhari (1284, 6655) and Muslim (923), on the authority of Usâmah ibn Zayd.

performed prostration, he placed her on the ground; and when he stood up for a new unit of the Prayer, he picked her up again.[45]

On another occasion, when the Prophet (ﷺ) went down to perform prostration during congregational Prayer, al-Ḥasan (ﷺ) climbed onto his back. The Prophet (ﷺ) then prolonged his prostration, and when he completed his Prayer, he apologized to the other members of the congregation and then said: "Verily, this son of mine (i.e., al-Ḥasan) climbed on top of me, and I disliked the idea of raising my head until he first descended (of his own volition)."[46]

The Prophet (ﷺ) exhorted his Companions to follow his example, saying to them: "When someone among you leads people (in Prayer), then let him shorten the length of his Prayer, for among the people are the elderly, the very young, the sick, and the ones who have important errands to do."[47]

Once, when Mu'âdh (ﷺ), while leading others, prolonged the length of his Prayer, the Prophet (ﷺ) said to him: "O Mu'âdh, are you a *Fattân*!"[48] A *Fattân* is someone who puts others to trial, or who tempts them away from what they should be doing; in the context of this hadith, the Prophet (ﷺ) meant the following: "O Mu'âdh, are you discouraging people from coming to perform Congregational Prayer?" The Prophet (ﷺ) even refrained from

---

[45] Related by Bukhari (516) and Muslim (543), on the authority of Abu Qatâdah.

[46] Related by Aḥmad (27100) and Nasâ'i (1141), on the authority of Shaddâd ibn al-Hâd.

[47] Related by Bukhari (703) and Muslim (468), on the authority of Abu Hurayrah.

[48] Related by Bukhari (705, 6106) and Muslim (465), on the authority of Jâbir ibn 'Abdullâh.

making certain recommended practices into laws because he didn't want to make matters difficult for Muslims; for example, he said, "Had doing so not been difficult for the people, I would have ordered them to use *Siwâk* (a stick that is used to clean one's teeth) at the time of every Prayer."[49]

The Prophet (ﷺ) would say to his Companions, "Moderation, moderation — and then you will reach (your goal of safety, salvation, etc.)."[50] He would also say, "I have been sent with *al-Ḥaneefiyah as-Samḥah*."[51] Or in other words, "I have been sent with a Religion that rejects falsehood and promotes pure Monotheism, a Religion that is tolerant, lenient, and easy to follow." He would also say, "The best of your Religion is the easiest of it."[52] He was also known to say, "Follow a moderate guidance."[53]

The Prophet (ﷺ) said: "Do, in terms of deeds, only that which you can handle; for indeed, Allah does not become bored until you become bored."[54] Of course, 'boredom' is a quality that is not befitting of Allah's greatness, perfection, and Majesty; therefore, some of the people of knowledge have interpreted the phrase "Allah does not become bored" as follows: "He (ﷺ) does not treat you as one who becomes bored would treat you, by cutting you off from His rewards; instead, as long as you do not

---

[49] Related by Bukhari (887) and Muslim (252), on the authority of Abu Hurayrah.

[50] Related by Bukhari (6463), on the authority of Abu Hurayrah.

[51] Related by Aḥmad (21788), on the authority of Abu Umâmah.

[52] Related by Aḥmad (15506); refer to *Majmâ' az-Zawâid* (3/308).

[53] Related by Aḥmad (22454, 22544); and by Bayhaqi, in *as-Sunan al-Kubrâ* (4519), on the authority of Buraydah al-Aslami. Refer to *al-Bayân wat-Ta'reef* (2/109).

[54] Related by Bukhari (5862) and Muslim (782), on the authority of 'Â'ishah.

become bored of doing good deeds, He will not stop bestowing upon you His rewards."

Whenever the Prophet (ﷺ) was given two choices, he would choose the easier of the two, as long as doing so did not involve sinning. On one occasion, he reproached three men who imposed upon themselves strict and unreasonable rules for worshipping Allah. They felt that, since, unlike the Prophet (ﷺ), their past and future sins had not been forgiven, they would have to perform more acts of worship than even the Prophet (ﷺ) performed. One of them vowed to spend the whole of every night of his life in prayer; another made an oath to fast every day; and the third one among them vowed never to marry. The Prophet (ﷺ) said to them: "By Allah, I fear Allah and am afraid of Him to a greater degree than any person among you. And yet I stand up (to pray) and I sleep; I fast (some days), and I don't fast (other days). So whosoever turns away from my Sunnah (my way, my guidance, etc.) is not from me."[55]

The Prophet (ﷺ) understood that travelling was an ordeal in and of itself — given that a traveller has to forsake his home for an extended period of time, that he must endure the heat of the sun, that his sleep schedule becomes disturbed, and so on. Therefore, in order to make matters easy for his people, the Prophet (ﷺ) legislated certain practices — or established certain precedents — that made travelling a less trying ordeal: While travelling during Ramaḍân, he would sometimes abstain from fasting; he would shorten the length of four-unit Prayers; he would join between the _Dhuhr_ and _'Aṣr_ Prayers, and between the _Maghrib_ and _'Isha'_

---

[55] Related by Bukhari (5063) and Muslim (1401), on the authority of Anas ibn Mâlik.

Prayers. And on a rainy day, his *Mu'adh-dhin* (the man who made the call to Prayer) called out to the people, saying, "Pray in your homes."

Gentleness, moderation, and consistency — these were all qualities that the Prophet (ﷺ) encouraged his followers to adopt. Harshness, immoderation, and inconsistency — these were all qualities that the Prophet (ﷺ) shunned. According to one narration, the Prophet (ﷺ) said: "Whenever gentleness is found in something, it adorns that thing; whenever it is removed from something, then that thing becomes sullied and tainted."[56] According to another narration, the Prophet (ﷺ) reproached 'Abdullâh ibn 'Amr ibn al-'Âṣ (ﷺ) for overburdening himself with too many acts of worship. He (Blessings and peace be upon him) said, "Beware of immoderation."[57]

It is related that the Prophet (ﷺ) said: "My Nation is a Nation that has mercy on it."[58] He also said, "When I give you a command, follow it as much as you are able to."[59] The ease the Prophet (ﷺ) promoted through his personal example is the very ease that Allah, the Exalted, Almighty promotes in various verses of His Book:

(سورة الأعلى : ٨)   ﴿وَنُيَسِّرُكَ لِلْيُسْرَىٰ ۝﴾

[56] Related by Muslim (2594), on the authority of 'Â'ishah.

[57] Related by Aḥmad (1854, 3238); Nasâ'i (3057); Ibn Mâjah (3029); and Ibn Abi 'Âṣim, in *as-Sunnah* (1/46), on the authority of Ibn 'Abbâs. And Ibn Abi 'Âṣim declared this hadith to be authentic.

[58] Related by Aḥmad (19179, 19253); Abu Dâwood (4278); and al-Ḥâkim (8372), on the authority of Abu Moosa. And al-Ḥâkim declared this hadith to be authentic.

[59] Related by Bukhari (7288) and Muslim (1337), on the authority of Abu Hurayrah.

❨And We shall make easy for you [O Muhammad] the easy way [i.e., the doing of righteous deeds].❩ *(Qur'an 87: 8)*

(سورة البَقَرَة: ٢٨٦) ❨ ۞ ... ﴿لَا يُكَلِّفُ ٱللَّهُ نَفْسًا إِلَّا وُسْعَهَا ❩

❨Allah burdens not a person beyond his scope...❩ *(Qur'an 2: 286)*

(سورة التَّغَابُن: ١٦) ❨ ۞ ... ﴿فَٱتَّقُوا ٱللَّهَ مَا ٱسْتَطَعْتُمْ ❩

❨So keep your duty to Allah and fear Him as much as you can...❩ *(Qur'an 64: 16)*

(سورة البَقَرَة: ١٨٥) ❨ ۞ ... يُرِيدُ ٱللَّهُ بِكُمُ ٱلْيُسْرَ وَلَا يُرِيدُ بِكُمُ ٱلْعُسْرَ ... ﴿ ❩

❨... Allah intends for you ease, and He does not want to make things difficult for you...❩ *(Qur'an 2: 185)*

(سورة الحَجّ: ٧٨) ❨ ۞ ... وَمَا جَعَلَ عَلَيْكُمْ فِي ٱلدِّينِ مِنْ حَرَجٍ ... ﴿ ❩

❨... And He has not laid upon you in religion any hardship...❩ *(Qur'an 22: 78)*

His Remembrance of Allah

It is related that, in a single gathering, the Prophet (ﷺ) asked Allah for forgiveness seventy times. That is certainly indicative of the degree to which the Prophet (ﷺ) remembered Allah. The fact is that no person has ever, or will ever, remember Allah as much as the Prophet (ﷺ) remembered Him.

The entire life of the Prophet (ﷺ) involved the remembrance of Allah. Inviting others to Islam, delivering speeches, gaving advice, performing acts of worship, fighting on the battlefield, issuing legal rulings — everything the Prophet (ﷺ) did involved the remembrance of Allah (ﷻ). The Prophet (ﷺ) remembered Allah both by day and by night, when at home and when away on a journey. Every breath he took involved the remembrance of Allah. Even his sleep was not bereft of the remembrance of Allah, for while his eyes slept, his heart remained awake. His heart was attached to his Lord. He personified piety and righteousness to such a great extent that, just to look at him reminded people of their Lord.

He would encourage Muslims to remember their Lord as well, saying to them: " 'The *Mufarradoon* have preceded (or beat) (others).' His Companions asked him to explain the meaning of the word *Mufarradoon*, and he replied, '(*Al-Mufarradoon* are) the men and women who remember Allah a great deal.' "[60] According to another narration, he said, "The example of the person who remembers his Lord and the person who does not remember Him, is that of the living and the dead."[61] Once, when a man asked for advice, the Prophet (ﷺ) said to him: "Let your tongue remain moist with the remembrance of Allah."[62]

The more one remembers Allah (ﷻ), the better one is as a Muslim. In a *Qudsee* hadith, the Prophet (ﷺ) related that Allah said: "I am with My slave as long as he remembers Me, and as

---

[60] Related by Muslim (2676), on the authority of Abu Hurayrah.

[61] Related by Bukhari (6407) and Muslim (779), on the authority of Abu Moosa.

[62] Related by Aḥmad (17227, 17245), Tirmidhi (3375) and Ibn Mâjah (3793). Refer to *al-Mishkât al-Maṣâbeeḥ* (2279).

long as his lips move (with remembrance of Me)."[63] In another *Qudsee* hadith, Allah said: "If one remembers Me to himself, I remember him to My Self. If one remembers Me in a gathering, I remember him in a gathering that is better than it."[64]

There are numerous narrations in which the Prophet (ﷺ) encouraged Muslims to remember Allah; in many of those narrations, he encouraged Muslims to repeatedly and frequently utter specific, important phrases of remembrance — such as the phrase of *Tawheed*, "None has the right to be worshipped but Allah"; phrases in which a person glorifies Allah, such as the saying, "*Subhânallâh* (How perfect Allah is!)"; phrases of praise, such as the saying, "*Alhamdulillâh* (All praise is for Allah)"; phrases with which one magnifies Allah, such as the saying, "*Allâhu akbar* (Allah is the greatest)"; the *al-Hawqalah* phrase, "There is neither might nor power except with Allah (*Lâ Hawla walâ Quwwata Illa Billâh*)"; phrases with which one asks Allah for forgiveness, such as the saying, "O Allah, forgive me (*Astaghfirullâh*)"; and phrases with which one invokes Allah to send prayers and salutations upon Prophet Muhammad (ﷺ).

Entire volumes of books can be written on the topic of remembrance, for the Prophet (ﷺ) spoke frequently about the various aspects of remembering Allah — such as the phrases of remembrance that one should utter, phrases of remembrance that are specific to certain occasions, phrases of remembrance that believers should consistently utter in the morning and evening, the

---

[63] Bukhari related it as a *Mu'âllaq* narration in the "Book of *Tawheed*." This narration is also related by Ahmad (10585, 10592) and Ibn Mâjah (3792), on the authority of Abu Hurayrah.

[64] Related by Bukhari (7405) and Muslim (2675), on the authority of Abu Hurayrah.

benefits of remembering Allah, the rewards one receives for remembering Allah, and so on.

Before teaching others about the importance of remembering Allah, the Prophet (ﷺ) first set a good example himself, remembering Allah at all times, and on all occasions. And when he would remember Allah, he would do so with a fearful, attentive, and observant heart — a heart that was filled with the emotions of fear, love, and hope; a heart that ardently desired achieving the Good Pleasure of Allah (ﷻ).

The Prophet Doing Supplication

Before reading on about *Du'â'* (supplication), the reader would do well to understand the basic differences and commonalities between the terms *Du'â'*, or supplication; *Ṣalâh*, or Prayer; and *'Ibâdah*, or worship. *Ṣalâh* refers specifically to a regulated form of worship, one that involves standing, bowing, prostrating, and sitting down; and that also involves magnifying Allah, reciting the Qur'an, glorifying Allah, and sending Prayers upon the Prophet (ﷺ). *Du'â'* involves supplicating to Allah — by asking Him for help, guidance, prosperity, rewards, Paradise, etc. One can make *Du'â'* at any time, even during certain parts of Prayer (*Ṣalâh*), such as when one is performing prostration. *'Ibâdah*, or worship, is a more universal term, in that it applies to any and all acts of worship. If we have the right intention, we can transform any action or deed into an act of worship. Therefore, *'Ibâdah* is not limited to Prayer (*Ṣalâh*), though it does comprehend it. Prayer is *'Ibâdah* (worship), and so too is *Du'â'* (supplication). The Prophet (ﷺ) said: "*Ad-Du'â' is 'Ibâdah.*"[65]

In regard to supplication, Allah (ﷻ) said:

$$﴿وَقَالَ رَبُّكُمُ ٱدْعُونِىٓ أَسْتَجِبْ لَكُمْ ... ﴿٦٠﴾﴾$$

(سورة غَافِر: ٦٠)

﴾And your Lord said, 'Invoke Me, [i.e., believe in My Oneness (Islamic Monotheism)] [and ask Me for anything] I will respond to your [invocation]...﴿   *(Qur'an 40: 60)*

In another verse, Allah (ﷻ) said:

$$﴿وَإِذَا سَأَلَكَ عِبَادِى عَنِّى فَإِنِّى قَرِيبٌ أُجِيبُ دَعْوَةَ ٱلدَّاعِ إِذَا دَعَانِ ... ﴿١٨٦﴾﴾$$

(سورة البَقَرَة: ١٨٦)

﴾And when My slaves ask you [O Muhammad] concerning Me, then [answer them], I am indeed near [to them by My Knowledge]. I respond to the invocations of the supplicant when he calls on Me [without any mediator or intercessor]...﴿   *(Qur'an 2: 186)*

The more people ask a fellow human being for help, the more he becomes angry, feeling that they are taking advantage of his generosity. The opposite is true for Allah (ﷻ): The more people ask Him for help, the more pleased He becomes with them; and conversely, the less people ask Him for help, the less pleased He becomes with them. The Prophet (ﷺ) said: "If one does not ask Allah (for help, for guidance, etc.), Allah becomes angry with him."[66]

---

[65] Related by Aḥmad (17888, 17919), Abu Dâwood (1479), and Tirmidhi (2969, 3247), on the authority of an-Nuʿmân ibn Basheer. And Tirmidhi declared this hadith to be authentic.

[66] Related by Bukhari, in *al-Adab al-Mufrad* (658); and by Tirmidhi (3373), on the authority of Abu Hurayrah. Tirmidhi ruled that this hadith is authentic.

The Prophet (ﷺ) depended on no one save Allah; and in Allah, he placed his complete trust. Consequently, he invoked Allah for help at all times and on all occasions. Anything he wanted, he asked for from Allah. Among other things, he asked for Allah's mercy, forgiveness, and rewards.

Although the Prophet (ﷺ) did ask for specific things, his supplications generally consisted of few words that embraced a number of rewards and blessings. For instance, what supplication can be more comprehensive than the following one that the Prophet (ﷺ) taught us: "O Allah, give us that which is good in this life and that which is good in the Hereafter, and protect us from the punishment of the Hellfire."[67] In another supplication, the Prophet (ﷺ) said: "O Allah, I ask you for pardon and well-being"[68] — a comprehensive supplication with which the Prophet (ﷺ) asked for well-being both of the spiritual and the physical kind.

The Prophet (ﷺ) would repeat his supplications three times; before supplication, he would praise and extol Allah; while supplicating, he would face the *Qiblah* (the direction of the Ka'bah); and at times, he would perform ablution before supplicating. He would teach these and other etiquettes of supplication to his followers — for instance, instructing them to ask Allah (ﷻ) by His Beautiful Names, to be persistent in their supplications, and to thus never despair of having their supplications answered. The Prophet (ﷺ) further instructed his

---

[67] Related by Bukhari (4522, 6389) and Muslim (2688), on the authority of Anas.

[68] Related by Aḥmad (4770), Abu Dâwood (5074), Ibn Mâjah (3871), and al-Ḥâkim (1902), on the authority of Ibn 'Umar. And al-Ḥâkim ruled that this hadith is authentic.

followers to supplicate on specific occasions, occasions on which supplications are more likely to be answered: At the conclusion of Prayer; between the *Adhân* (the call to Prayer) and the *Iqâmah* (the shorter, final call to the commencement of Prayer); during the last hour of Friday; the Day of 'Arafah; and while one is fasting, travelling, or performing prostration. The Prophet (ﷺ) also indicated the special strength and potency of a father's supplications for his child.

The Prophet (ﷺ) invoked Allah on all occasions; but during times of crisis, he increased the intensity of his supplications, repeatedly turning to Allah for help, feeling all the while a sense of fear, humility, and love; furthermore, he had good thoughts about Allah and a strong sense of hope that Allah would answer his Prayers — as Allah most certainly did on many occasions, such as the days of Badr, Khandaq, and 'Arafah; the day the Prophet (ﷺ) stood on the pulpit and prayed for rain, immediately after which rain began to fall down in abundance; and the day Allah (ﷻ) caused the moon to split into two pieces.

The Prophet (ﷺ) benefited greatly from his supplications, for Allah blessed him in his wealth, his food, and his drink. Allah supported him in his wars, granting victory to him and his followers and inflicting his enemies with humiliating defeats. And Allah continued to help him and answer his Prayers until he departed from this world, having accomplished all that he had set out to accomplish and much more besides.

The Prophet's lofty ambitions

To be ambitious is to have an ardent desire for distinction; however, most often the word 'ambition' is used in a negative sense — to refer to someone who has an inordinate desire for distinction, to someone who is willing to do anything, even immoral acts, to succeed in life. But diametrically opposed to one another are the ambitions of most men when compared with the ambitions of the Prophet (ﷺ). Most ambitious men are determined to become rich and powerful in this world; the Prophet's ambitions, on the other hand, were focused on the life to come. That, essentially, is what made his ambitions so unique.

It is as if lofty ambitions and noble aspirations came out with the Prophet (ﷺ) as he exited from his mother's womb. From a very young age, the Prophet (ﷺ) strove to achieve the higher aims of life — such as moral rectitude, sound beliefs, and good manners. Everyone around him perceived in him a budding lofty character. His grandfather, 'Abdul-Muṭṭalib, would sit on a specific carpet in front of the Ka'bah; because of his status among the Quraysh, no one else dared to sit on it, not even 'Abdul-Muṭṭalib's children. But the Prophet (ﷺ) did dare to sit on it alongside his grandfather, who actually encouraged him, by allowing him to sit on it, while he did not allow his own children to do the same.

The Prophet (ﷺ) was a natural-born leader, a man, who, because of his character, gained the universal respect of all who knew him. Thus, even before the Prophet (ﷺ) received revelation for the very first time, his fellow tribesmen would call him "The Truthful One", and "The Trustworthy One". They trusted him so much that they would leave their valuable possessions with no one but him; and they trusted in his wisdom and judgment so much that they would go to him and ask him to resolve their disputes.

If the Messenger of Allah (ﷺ) aspired to excellence during his youth, he, upon actually becoming a Prophet, came to aspire to even greater things. For upon becoming a Prophet, the Messenger of Allah (ﷺ) yearned not for wealth, power, or worldly status, but for what is known as *al-Waseelah*, which is the highest ranking in Paradise. So much did the Prophet (ﷺ) aspire to that ranking that he asked his followers to pray that he be granted it.

Through having good and noble ambitions, the Prophet (ﷺ) became a complete and ideal human being. And because of his lofty ambitions, he had neither the time nor the desire to hanker after the insignificant treasures, palaces, fame, and power of this fleeting and temporary abode. These days, people are encouraged to 'aim high'; no one, however, can claim to aim higher than the Prophet (ﷺ), who not only desired, but also worked for, the highest possible ranking in the Hereafter.

The Messenger of Allah (ﷺ) in the Qur'an:

(سورة الأنفال: ٦٤)   ﴿يَٰٓأَيُّهَا ٱلنَّبِىُّ حَسْبُكَ ٱللَّهُ ... ﴿٦٤﴾﴾

﴿O Prophet [Muhammad]! Allah is sufficient for you...﴾*(Qur'an 8: 64)*

When something or someone is sufficient for a person, it means that that thing or person is adequate for a certain purpose; or that that thing or person is enough to achieve a goal, whereby no other thing or person is also necessary for that goal. Bearing that in mind, the reader would do well to ask the question, how was Allah (ﷻ) sufficient for the Prophet (ﷺ)?

When Allah (ﷻ) said: "O Prophet (Muhammad), Allah is sufficient for you," it was as if Allah was saying the following to him: "Allah is sufficient for you regarding every aspect of your life, such that you will need no one else for help or assistance. Allah protected you in times of crises, took care of you during times of hardship, and guarded you during the most gloomy of times. Therefore, be not afraid; be not sad; and be not anxious or nervous."

Allah (ﷻ) is your Helper against every enemy, your source of aid against every opponent, your supporter in every affair. When you ask for anything, He gives you. When you ask for forgiveness, He forgives you. When you are thankful to Him, He gives you an increase of blessings. When you remember Him, He remembers you. When you fight against your enemy, He grants you victory. And when you make a decision or a judgment in any given matter, He guides you to what is right.

Allah (ﷻ) is sufficient for you: He grants you honor when you have no family to help you; He makes you rich without the need for money; and He protects you without the use of guards. You are granted victory because Allah is sufficient for you. You are guided to what is right because Allah is sufficient for you. And because Allah is sufficient for you, you need not fear the evil eye of the jealous one, the plotting of your enemy, the deception of the treacherous, the wickedness of the disbeliever, and the trickery of the conniving evil-doer.

When you hear about the onslaught of the enemy, the threats of your foes, the evil plots of the hypocrites, or the gloating of jealous ones over your misfortunes — remain steadfast, for indeed, Allah (ﷻ) is sufficient for you.

When times are hard, when relatives turn their backs on you, when friends begin to lose hope of victory, and when help is slow in coming — remain steadfast, for indeed, Allah (ﷻ) is sufficient for you.

When calamity descends upon you, when tragedy strikes you, and when you are surrounded by misfortune and the threat of utter destruction — remain steadfast, for indeed, Allah is sufficient for you. During such times, do not turn to people for help, and do not rely on anyone save Allah (ﷻ), for indeed, He is sufficient for you.

When sickness befalls you, when debts weigh down on you, when poverty brings you down, when you need something you cannot get — then do not be sad, for indeed, Allah (ﷻ) is sufficient for you.

When help is slow in coming, when victory is delayed, and when a calamity seems too much to bear — do not be sad, for indeed, Allah (ﷻ) is sufficient for you. *O Muhammad, you are protected because you are My Khaleel (a relationship that denotes the highest form of love). You are under My Care because you are My Messenger. And you will always remain under My Divine Protection because you are My chosen slave, My chosen Prophet.*

(سورة التوبة : ٤٠)   ﴿ ... لَا تَحْزَنْ إِنَّ ٱللَّهَ مَعَنَا ... ﴾

﴾... And be not sad [or afraid], surely Allah is with us...﴿

(Qur'an 9: 40)

These brave, dignified, and peaceful words were spoken by the Prophet (ﷺ), at a time when he was alone in a cave with his Companion Abu Bakr aṣ-Ṣiddeeq (ﷺ), and when his enemies had him surrounded. He did not tremble when he said them, his lips did not falter, and he did not speak with a fearful stutter; instead, he uttered them with a firm resolve, with an unwavering belief that "Allah is with us."

In saying those words, it was as if the Prophet (ﷺ) was saying the following to Abu Bakr (رضي الله عنه): "As long as Allah is with us, then why the sadness? Why the fear? Why the anxiousness? Be at peace, be firm, and be calm, for Allah is with us."

"Since Allah (ﷻ) is with us, we will not fail, we will not be defeated, we will not be forsaken, and we will not have cause to lose hope. Victory and ultimate success is ours because Allah is with us.

Since Allah is with us, who can be stronger than us? Who can be better-guided than us? Who can be more hopeful of His Help?

Our enemies are weak; our opponents are cowards; our foes will falter — all of these things are true because Allah is with us. We will seek help from no human being, we will pray to no man, we will fear no created being because, and only because, Allah (ﷻ) is with us.

We are braver, our weapons are more effective, and our way is more upright because Allah is with us. We are the mightier, we are the stronger, we are the more honored, we are the ones who will be helped — there is no doubt about these realities since Allah (ﷻ) is with us.

O Abu Bakr, cast off your gloom, do not be sad, and forget your worries and troubles — for Allah (ﷻ) is with us.

O Abu Bakr, raise your head, calm your nerves, be at peace in your heart — for Allah (ﷻ) is with us.

O Abu Bakr, expect help, eagerly anticipate divine intervention, and receive glad tidings of imminent success — for indeed, Allah (ﷻ) is with us.

O Abu Bakr, tomorrow our message will spread far and wide, our Religion will be victorious, and our voices will be heard — for indeed, Allah (ﷻ) is with us.

O Abu Bakr, tomorrow the people of earth will hear the majestic sound of the *Adhân* (the call to Prayer), the wonderful speech of the Most-Merciful, the beautiful rhythm of the Qur'an — all of this will come to pass because Allah (ﷻ) is with us.

O Abu Bakr, tomorrow we will take mankind out of the darkness of disbelief, we will bring them into the light of Faith, we will save them from the shackles of slavery to created beings, and allow them to enjoy the freedom of being slaves to none but Allah — and again, this will indeed happen because Allah (ﷻ) is with us!"

(٤ :سورة القَلَم) ﴿وَإِنَّكَ لَعَلَىٰ خُلُقٍ عَظِيمٍ ۝﴾

﴾And verily, you [O Muhammad] are on an exalted standard of character.﴿ *(Qur'an 68: 4)*

O Muhammad, you are, by Allah, upon an exalted standard of character. You are a paragon of modesty and nobility. If the character you displayed outside in public was noble, your private, secret life was even better. All noble qualities you possessed in the highest degree. Your enemies wronged you, and you remained patient; they hurt you, and you forgave them; they cursed you, and you pardoned them; they were rude to you, and you overlooked their shortcomings. In short, you are, O Muhammad, as Allah described you to be — 'upon an exalted standard of character'.

You are loved by all kinds of people: kings and common citizens, the young and the old, men and women, the rich and the poor, relatives and non-relatives. They all love you because you won over their hearts with your compassion, and because you enraptured their souls with your noble qualities and good manners.

Revelation served to refine your character; your Lord guided you; Jibreel taught you; and Allah's protection and care accompanied your every breath, your every thought, your every movement, and your every action. Consequently, Allah (﷾) blessed you by guiding you to be 'upon a high standard of character'.

A smile could always be seen on your face, light could be discerned on your forehead, love emanated from your heart, and your hand was the giving hand of generosity. In short, you were blessed in every possible way.

Even if a sword was held threateningly your head, you still would not lie. Even if someone were to tempt you with a promise of the world's treasures, you still would not act treacherously. And even if you were offered a vast kingdom, you still would not betray your principles. You would not do any of those things because you are a divinely-protected Prophet, and because you were sent to be an ideal example for all of mankind.

You remained 'upon an exalted standard of character' even when you were threatened by death; you remained brave even when you were challenged by the most skilled of fighters; and you were generous even when you were asked to give away all that you owned. You surpassed all of the world's inhabitants — from the past, present, and future — in your piety, modesty, generosity, bravery, trustworthiness, knowledge, and every other fathomable noble quality. O Muhammad, you are, without a doubt, 'upon an exalted standard of character'.

(سورة القَلَم : ٢) ﴿وَمَآ أَنتَ بِنِعۡمَةِ رَبِّكَ بِمَجۡنُونٍ ۝﴾

❨You [O Muhammad] are not, by the Grace of your Lord, a madman.❩ *(Qur'an 68: 2)*

Contrary to what your enemies have said about you, you are not a madman; in fact, you are not only of sound mind yourself, you have come with the cure for all mental ailments. The true madman, the veritable deranged person is the one who rejects you, opposes you, disbelieves in you, and wages war against you. ❨You [O Muhammad] are not, by the Grace of your Lord, a madman.❩ *(Qur'an 68: 2)*

How can you be mad when you are the sanest, wisest, noblest, and most intelligent of people? You have come with revelation, revelation that removes falsehood, exposes misguidance, erases ignorance, and guides the mind. Because you are guided by your Lord, because you are certain of your way, because Allah cares for your spiritual and physical well-being, because you follow clear and logical proofs — because of all these reasons, it is clear that you are certainly not mad. You are, after all, the one who teaches the most knowledgeable of the knowledgeable from among human beings, the most rightly-guided of the rightly-guided, and the wisest of the wise.

He has certainly lied, therefore, who describes you as being mad or insane. You have filled the world with wisdom, guidance, and justice. If wisdom is not found with you, then where else can it be found? How could people have claimed that you are mad when you have left mankind with the best and most valuable of legacies? An Arab poet rightly said about you:

Your brother Jesus called out to a dead man,

who then rose up for him,

Meanwhile you gave life to generations

upon generations of people.

◆And verily, you [O Muhammad] are indeed guiding [mankind] to the Straight Path [i.e., Allah's Religion of Islamic Monotheism].◆

(Qur'an 42: 52)

O Muhammad, your mission in life is to guide, and your duty is to educate and raise people from the abyss of immorality to the heights of guidance and uprightness.

You, and you alone, guide people to the Straight Path. Therefore, if any person wants to be happy, he must follow you; if any person wants ultimate success, he must obey you; and if any person desires safety and salvation, he must follow your guidance.

The best of Prayers is your Prayer; the best fasting is your fasting; the most complete Ḥajj (Pilgrimage to Makkah) is your Ḥajj; the purest and most beneficial charity is the charity you gave; and the most excellent remembrance is your remembrance of Allah (﷽).

◆And verily, you [O Muhammad] are indeed guiding [mankind] to the Straight Path.◆: Whoever boards the ship of your guidance will be led to the shores of safety and salvation. Whoever enters the sanctuary of your message will be safe from all perils. Whoever follows your guidance will be saved from ultimate humiliation. How can a follower of yours suffer humiliation when victory is your constant companion? And how can a follower of yours go astray when you are the source of true guidance?

Verily, you guide the mind, thus saving it from falsehood; with your message, you purify the mind, thus protecting it from doubts; with your wise words, you cleanse the soul, thus protecting it from betrayal and treachery. You have taken this Nation out of darkness, and you have freed mankind from being slaves to other slaves, by making them slaves only unto Allah (ﷻ).

You are the embodiment of true guidance: Your speech is guidance, your demeanor is guidance, and your every action is a manifestation of true guidance. You guide people unto Allah (ﷻ); you show them the way of righteousness; you lead them to every good and noble deed; and you invite them to Paradise.

﴾ ۞ يَـٰٓأَيُّهَا ٱلرَّسُولُ بَلِّغْ مَآ أُنزِلَ إِلَيْكَ مِن رَّبِّكَ ... ﴿٦٧﴾ ﴾ (سورة المَائدة: ٦٧)

﴾O Messenger [Muhammad]! Proclaim [the Message] which has been sent down to you from your Lord.﴿ *(Qur'an 5: 67)*

O Muhammad, just as you have heard the message of Islam in its entirety, convey it in its entirety. Leave out no sentence, no word, and no letter. This message is a trust, and you will be questioned about it. Convey both the exact words of the message and the spirit of the message. Convey the revelation that has descended upon you.

You are simply a conveyor of this message. It is, therefore, neither your job nor your right to add anything to it or to remove anything from it. You are sent on a precise, predetermined mission, so carry out that mission precisely as it was dictated to you.

Regardless of who accepts or rejects your message, and regardless of who follows you or turns away from you, convey the message that was revealed to you from your Lord. The carrying out of your mission does not hinge upon any worldly occurrence; or in other words, no matter what happens, remain focused on the task at hand — which is to fulfill your duty of conveying the message of Islam to all of mankind.

Convey your message to everyone, and advise everyone — the haughty and the weak, masters and slaves, human beings and jinns, men and women, the rich and the poor, the old and the young.

Convey what has been revealed to you: Do so without fearing your enemies; without being afraid of a menacing sword or near-certain death; and without betraying your principles as a result of being in awe of an approaching, powerful army.

Convey what has been revealed to you, and do not allow wealth to tempt you, power to corrupt you, status to entice you, or worldly possessions to beguile you.

﴿ ... وَإِن لَّمْ تَفْعَلْ فَمَا بَلَّغْتَ رِسَالَتَهُ ۚ ... ﴿٦٧﴾ ﴾   (سورة المائدة: ٦٧)

❨... And if you do not [proclaim the message that has been sent down to you from your Lord], then you have not conveyed His Message...❩

(Qur'an 5: 67)

Or in other words, 'if you do not convey the message (of Islam) in its entirety, then you have not accomplished anything'. If you hide any part of it, or keep to yourself any verse, sentence, or phrase from it, then you have not truly conveyed the message of your Lord, and you have not fulfilled what Allah has entrusted you with. We [i.e., Allah (﷾)] want you to convey the message to people the same way that Jibreel (ﷺ) came down and conveyed it to you.

﴿ ... وَٱللَّهُ يَعْصِمُكَ مِنَ ٱلنَّاسِ ... ﴾ ⟨٦٧⟩ (سورة المَائدة: ٦٧)

❨... Allah will protect you from mankind...❩ *(Qur'an 5: 67)*

Convey the message of your Lord, and, while doing so, be afraid of no person. How can you fear people, when I am with you, helping you, taking care of you, defending you, and protecting you from mankind? No one will kill you, for I am protecting you from mankind. No one will extinguish your light, for I am protecting you from mankind. No one will hinder your progress, for I am protecting you from mankind. Openly proclaim the message you have been entrusted with. Be afraid of no created being, for I am protecting you from mankind.

There is no power or strength on earth that can defeat you; there is no standing army on earth that can kill you; there is no king or emperor who can subjugate you. Therefore, go forth and proclaim the message of Islam, being certain that you will always be blessed with the protection of your Lord (ﷻ).

﴿ ۞ أَلَمْ نَشْرَحْ لَكَ صَدْرَكَ ⟨١⟩ ﴾ (سورة الشَّرح: ١)

❨Have We not opened your breast for you [O Muhammad]?❩
(Qur'an 94: 1)

'Have We not opened your breast, O Muhammad', making you caring, merciful, and compassionate? Have We not opened your breast and filled it with light and happiness, making it wide and expansive as opposed to narrow and small and confined? Have We not opened your breast and filled it with wisdom, Faith, mercy, and goodness?

Have We not opened your breast, making you a large-hearted person — a person who forgives the transgressions of others; who overlooks people's faults; who conceals people's weaknesses; who is forbearing with foolish people; who, with an awe-inspiring level of dignity, turns away from ignorant people; and who is merciful towards weak and needy people.

We have opened your breast, thus making you like a good and gracious wind: generous and beneficial to all who encounter you. When people come to you for help, you never say 'no', but instead give with the generosity of a man who does not fear poverty.

We have opened your breast, so that it has become coolness and peace for you, extinguishing the effects of hurtful and rude speech, such that you reciprocate that speech with forgiveness and forbearance.

We have opened your breast, so that you are patient with the rudeness of Bedouins, the inane attacks of foolish people, the haughty speech of ignorant people, the spiteful speech of jealous people, and the gloating of enemies who take pleasure in your misfortunes.

We have opened your breast, so that you smile during crises, and are content during the harshest of times. And you remain firm and steadfast when calamities befall you.

We have opened your breast, so that you are not harsh and stern, but are instead merciful, compassionate, and gentle.

❨And removed from you your burden❩: We have washed you clean, removing all traces of your mistakes. You are forgiven for your past and future mistakes. Congratulations, therefore, for being thus forgiven! Congratulations for being honored with such great success!

❨Which weighed down your back?❩: The said burden weighed down your back, weakening it and causing it pain. But now We have removed from you that burden, so accept from Us that gift, and be happy with that honor.

❨And raised high your fame?❩: Whenever I am mentioned, you are mentioned alongside Me. Our names are inextricably juxtaposed: When I am mentioned, you too are mentioned during the *Adhân* (the call to Prayer), during Prayer, and during sermons and speeches. Could you ever hope for a greater honor than that? Every worshipper, every man and woman who glorifies Me, every person who performs Ḥajj, every *Khaṭeeb* (orator in general, deliverer of Friday sermons in particular) — mentions you. Are you seeking a distinction that is greater than that?

You are mentioned in both the Torah and the Injeel (the Gospel); you are honored and praised in the revealed scriptures of past nations.

We 'raised high your fame' so that it covers most parts of the earth like the rays of the sun. Across continents and seas the mention of your name travels at the speed of light. The inhabitants of every city know you; the people of every land have heard of you; the people of every village ask about you. You are discussed in gatherings both big and small.

We have 'raised high your fame' such that, even with the passing of many days and years, you are still not forgotten. Unlike scores of others, the mention of you has not been erased from the pages of history. Throughout history, countless men have made claims to glory, but who from them is remembered? And even if some of them are remembered, who still cares about them?

Even from the Muslim Nation, if people are remembered and revered, it is only because they followed you. Names of hadith narrators are memorized by students and scholars only because they had the honor of conveying to others your speech.

Entire civilizations have been lost due to the ravages of time, such that not a trace of them remains; and yet much more than your traces remain: The Book you came with in addition to your Sunnah remain intact and completely preserved. The glory of kings is gone, but your honor and distinction remain unchanged. Among human beings, no one's heart is as big as yours, no one's fame is raised as high as yours, and no one's biography is as rich and honorable as yours.

When a worshipper sits down and says the *Tashahud* (what is said by a worshipper during the sitting down phase of Prayer), he remembers not just Me, but you as well. When a worshipper stands up late at night to pray, he mentions not just Me, but you as well. When a *Khateeb* delivers his Friday sermon, he too mentions both Me and you. So praise your Lord, for We have indeed raised high your fame.

◖So verily, with the hardship, there is relief. Verily, with the hardship, there is relief [i.e., there is one hardship with two reliefs, so one hardship cannot overcome two reliefs].◗ When you are faced with a seemingly insurmountable problem, when there seems to be no escape from your problems, when a situation becomes almost unbearable, then know that relief and help and ease are near at hand.

Don't be sad, for after poverty comes richness; after illness comes good health; after suffering comes safety; after sadness comes happiness.

O Muhammad, you and your followers will indeed enjoy better days — days in which sustenance will be plentiful and victory will be yours.

It is a clearly established law in life that after hardship comes ease: night is followed by day; beyond the mountains of hardship are vast plains of comfort and ease; beyond the barren desert there is an expansive green garden.

Whenever a rope tightens, it snaps; and the same holds true for hardships: When a hardship becomes too hard to bear, it snaps, making way for ease, comfort, and better days. The traveller will soon find his home; the sick person will soon be cured; the prisoner will soon be released; the poor man will soon grow rich; the hungry man will soon become full; the thirsty man will soon have his thirst quenched; the sad man will soon have cause to be happy. In short, no matter what the situation, Allah (ﷻ) causes a hardship to be followed by ease.

The reader should note that this chapter was revealed during one of the most difficult periods of the Prophet's lifetime — a period of suffering, of being scorned by the nearest of relatives, and of being attacked by many enemies at once. The Prophet (ﷺ) needed to be consoled and comforted, and so Allah (ﷻ) revealed chapter *ash-Sharh* — a chapter that contains promises which were quickly fulfilled for the Messenger of Allah (ﷺ) and his Companions, and that therefore is a proof and a testament for people to contemplate until the Day of Resurrection. The chapter then continues:

❨So when you have finished [from your occupation], then stand up for Allah's worship [i.e., stand up for prayer].❩: When you are finished performing your worldly duties, and when you have taken care of personal errands, turn to Me in worship, remember Me, and supplicate to Me. When you have finished answering people's questions, come to My door, draw near to Me, and rub your forehead on the ground for My sake, so that you can achieve success, safety, and salvation.

When you have finished meeting with your family, your children, your relatives, and your wife, make time to spend with Me, time during which you present to Me your problems, ask Me for what you need, supplicate to Me for help, glorify Me, remember Me, and ask Me for forgiveness.

When you finish teaching and educating the people, come and ask, and you will be given more. I have a greater right over you than your own self has over you. I am more deserving of your free time than anyone else.

❨And to your Lord [Alone] turn [all your intentions and hopes and] your invocations.❩: Do not turn to anyone for help other than Me. To Me alone should you turn to for help, and in Me alone should you place your trust. Fear no one but Me, since I alone am able to punish wrongdoers; and place your hopes in no one but Me, for I alone give out rewards to good-doers. With Me are the keys to all treasures; therefore, I alone should be worshipped, and I alone should be supplicated to for help. So turn to Me, and I shall give you in abundance.

(سورة الفَتْح : ١) ❨إِنَّا فَتَحْنَا لَكَ فَتْحًا مُّبِينًا ❨١❩ ❩

❨Verily, We have given you [O Muhammad] a manifest victory.❩
(Qur'an 48: 1)

O Muhammad, we have given you a blessed, clear victory, a victory with which you won the hearts and minds of people. With that victory, you planted the seeds of Faith in the hearts of people; you conquered lands, so that true guidance spread wide and far. Through your message, I gave you victory — a victory in which the blind began to hear and the deaf began to hear. In fact, I caused your message to be heard by all human beings and jinns.

I granted you victory, and as a result of that, beneficial knowledge flowed from your tongue, and blessed guidance gushed forth from your heart. I granted you victory, and you gained, gathered, and then distributed the spoils of war.

We opened the door of knowledge to you, so that, while yesterday you were an illiterate man, today scholars come and take from your ocean of knowledge.

We granted you wealth, with which you gave generously to both relatives and strangers. You used the wealth I gave you to feed the hungry, clothe the naked, help the needy, and enrich the poor. You were able to do all of that by Our Grace, Mercy, and Generosity.

We granted you victory, helping you conquer cities and villages, and thus making your Religion reign supreme. In every aspect of your life, in every endeavor you have undertaken, in every situation you faced, I granted you guidance, help, and victory — so be thankful to no one but to Me.

(سورة محمد: ١٩)   ﴿فَٱعْلَمْ أَنَّهُ لَا إِلَٰهَ إِلَّا ٱللَّهُ ... ﴿١٩﴾﴾

﴿So know [O Muhammad] that Lâ ilâha illa-Allâh [none has the right to be worshipped but Allah]...﴾   (Qur'an 47: 19)

O Muhammad, now that you know that none has the right to be worshipped but Allah, do not associate any partners with Him in worship, and do not supplicate to anyone other than Him.

Instead, worship Him alone. When you ask for something, ask Allah; if you want help, seek it from Allah. None save Him can protect one from evil and harm, and none save Him can answer the prayers of one who is in need.

❴So know [O Muhammad] that *Lâ ilâha illa-Allâh* [none has the right to be worshipped but Allah]...❵ *(Qur'an 47: 19)*

It is His right that you worship Him alone, without associating any partners with Him in worship; that you fear Him; that you obey Him; and that you love Him.

❴So know [O Muhammad] that *Lâ ilâha illa-Allâh* [none has the right to be worshipped but Allah]...❵ *(Qur'an 47: 19)*

He (﷿) alone is perfect in His Beauty, Glory, and Majesty. He created human beings and jinns only so that they can worship Him. Whoever obeys Him gains His Good Pleasure; whoever loves Him gains His nearness; whoever fears Him becomes safe from His Punishment; and whoever glorifies Him becomes the beneficiary of His Generosity and Rewards. Conversely, whoever disobeys Him becomes the recipient of His Punishment; whoever wages war against Him is forsaken by Him; and whoever associates partners with Him in worship will be cast into the Hellfire. Allah (﷿) remembers those who remember Him; He gives an increase in blessings to those who are thankful to Him; and He humiliates those who disbelieve in Him. His is the dominion of the heavens and the earth, and to Him will you return for judgment.

❴So know [O Muhammad] that *Lâ ilâha illa-Allâh* [none has the right to be worshipped but Allah]...❵ *(Qur'an 47: 19)*

Devote yourself to worshipping Him alone, for He (﷿) does not accept any partner. And place your complete trust in Him, for He is All-Powerful and He is Sufficient for you as a Helper, Protector, and Guardian. Ask from Him alone, for He is the All-Rich. Fear His punishment, for His punishment is severe, agonizing, and painful to a degree unimaginable to any human being. Do not transgress His limits. And do not persecute or fight against His obedient slaves, for He exacts revenge on their behalf. Seek His forgiveness, for He is Merciful and Oft-Forgiving. Be Hopeful of receiving His rewards, for He is Generous. Seek refuge in His Sanctuary, for there you will find true safety. Remember Him often, so that you can gain His Love. Make it a habit, nay an addiction, to be thankful to Him; for if you are thankful to Him, He will give you an increase in rewards. Honor the things that He has made sacred in the Religion, and in so doing, you will gain His divine care and protection. And wage war against His enemies, for in so doing, you will be granted victory and great rewards.

(سورة العَلَق : ١)　　　　　　　　﴿أَقْرَأْ ... ۝﴾

{Read...}　　　　　　　　　　　　　　(Qur'an 96: 1)

The story of prophethood began with the word, "Read", on the day it was revealed to our Prophet (ﷺ) in the cave of Ḥirâ. So, in essence, the command to "read" was the launching point of our story, our history, and our life as a Nation. The day "read" was revealed, the world underwent a momentous change. The happiest part of our history as Muslims was the moment during which the command "read" was given to the Prophet (ﷺ): It was a defining moment for mankind, for it was a moment during which a clear distinction was made between darkness and light, disbelief and Faith, ignorance and knowledge.

Of all the words available in the Arabic lexicon, Allah (ﷻ) chose to begin the story of His Prophet's mission with the word "read". He did not say, "write", "pray", "speak", or "do good deeds". He chose to inaugurate His Prophet's mission with the simple, and yet highly significant, word, "read". So what is the secret behind Allah choosing that specific word? Well, it was as if Allah was saying the following: "O Muhammad, before you invite others to embrace Islam, read. And before you do good deeds, seek out knowledge."

(سورة محمّد: ١٩) ﴿... وَٱسۡتَغۡفِرۡ لِذَنۢبِكَ ﴿١٩﴾﴾ فَٱعۡلَمۡ أَنَّهُۥ لَآ إِلَٰهَ إِلَّا ٱللَّهُ

﴾So know [O' Muhammad] that Lâ ilâha illa-Allâh [none has the right to be worshipped but Allah], and ask forgiveness for your sin...﴿
(Qur'an 47: 19)

Reading is not to be a hobby, a diversion, or a pastime; on the contrary, it should be a way of life. It should be the goal of each person to cast off ignorance and to seek out beneficial knowledge.

May my mother and father be sacrificed for the Prophet (ﷺ)! Where should he have begun to read, given the fact that he never studied under the tutelage of a teacher, that he never read a book, and that he never even picked up a pen to write? He was commanded to begin by mentioning the name of His Lord, and by reading the speech of his Lord.

The word "read" points to the superiority and great importance of seeking out knowledge. Throughout the annals of history, anyone who has achieved happiness has done so as a result of having knowledge. What makes the Prophet's message so blessed is that it strikes a perfect balance between beneficial knowledge and noble actions. The Prophet (ﷺ) said: "The example of what Allah sent me with, in terms of guidance and knowledge, is the example of (beneficial) rain (that falls from the sky and causes crops to grow)."[69]

The Jews had knowledge but were without good deeds, and so Allah (ﷻ) became angry with them. The Christians performed good deeds, but they didn't have knowledge, and so they went astray. As for us, we have been commanded to seek refuge from both of their ways:

$$﴿صِرَٰطَ ٱلَّذِينَ أَنْعَمْتَ عَلَيْهِمْ غَيْرِ ٱلْمَغْضُوبِ عَلَيْهِمْ وَلَا ٱلضَّآلِّينَ ٧﴾$$

(سُورَة الفَاتِحَة : ٧)

❴Guide us to the Straight Way. The Way of those on whom You have bestowed Your Grace, not [the way] of those who earned Your Anger [such as the Jews], nor of those who went astray [such as the Christians].❵ *(Qur'an 1: 7)*

His crying

𝓘s crying a good or bad thing? Among men, the question is often asked, is it manly to cry? And when a man cries, is he being effeminate? Without a doubt, crying is not always a good thing. And there certainly are situations in which it is effeminate, or just downright foolish, for a man to cry. Nonetheless, certain

---

[69] Related by Bukhari (79) and Muslim (2282), on the authority of Abu Moosa al-Ash'ari.

situations call for crying; in fact, crying is actually a virtue in many situations.

It is a virtue to cry when one regrets having disobeyed Allah (ﷻ), or when one fears Allah's punishment in the Hereafter. It is a praiseworthy quality to cry when one remembers one's Lord, or when one fears the evil consequences of one's sins. In fact, crying in such situations is commendable, and is a proof of one's sincerity and piety. Allah (ﷻ) praised His Messenger for crying, saying:

﴿ ... إِذَا تُتْلَى عَلَيْهِمْ ءَايَتُ ٱلرَّحْمَـٰنِ خَرُّوا۟ سُجَّدًا وَبُكِيًّا ۩ ﴾ (سورة مَرِيَم: ٥٨)

◀... When the Verses of the Most Gracious [Allah] were recited unto them, they fell down prostrating and weeping.▶ *(Qur'an 19: 58)*

And Allah, the Exalted, the Almighty described His obedient slaves as follows:

﴿وَيَخِرُّونَ لِلْأَذْقَانِ يَبْكُونَ وَيَزِيدُهُمْ خُشُوعًا ۩ ﴾ (سورة الإسرَاء: ١٠٩)

◀And they fall down on their faces weeping and it adds to their humility.▶ *(Qur'an 17: 109)*

In another verse, Allah (ﷻ) condemned His enemies for being cold, unfeeling, and hard-hearted:

﴿أَفَمِنْ هَـٰذَا ٱلْحَدِيثِ تَعْجَبُونَ ۝ وَتَضْحَكُونَ وَلَا تَبْكُونَ ۝ ﴾(سورة النَّجم: ٥٩–٦٠)

◀Do you then wonder at this recital [the Qur'an]? And you laugh at it and weep not.▶ *(Qur'an 53: 59, 60)*

And in yet another verse, Allah (ﷻ) praised a group of people because of their sincerity and their crying:

﴿وَإِذَا سَمِعُوا مَا أُنزِلَ إِلَى ٱلرَّسُولِ تَرَىٰ أَعْيُنَهُمْ تَفِيضُ مِنَ ٱلدَّمْعِ مِمَّا عَرَفُوا مِنَ
ٱلْحَقِّ ... ﴾ (سورة المَائدة : ٨٣)

﴾And when they [who call themselves Christians] listen to what has
been sent down to the Messenger [Muhammad], you see their eyes
overflowing with tears because of the truth they have recognized...﴿
(Qur'an 5: 83)

The one man who feared Allah (ﷻ) to a greater degree than
anyone else was the Prophet (ﷺ). His heart was soft, and his eyes
were generous in shedding tears. He was so spiritually alive that
his eyelids constantly remained moist, always being on the verge
of crying. A thought about the Hereafter, a reminder about the
Hellfire, a word about Allah's Punishment — any of these things
would have quickly resulted in the Prophet (ﷺ) crying. When he
would recite the Qur'an, a sobbing sound could be heard from
him. In fact, his tears moved his Companions in ways that
speeches and sermons could never have done.

In the middle of one particular night, the Prophet (ﷺ) woke
up and proceeded to repeatedly recite the saying of Allah (ﷻ):

﴿إِن تُعَذِّبْهُمْ فَإِنَّهُمْ عِبَادُكَ وَإِن تَغْفِرْ لَهُمْ فَإِنَّكَ أَنتَ ٱلْعَزِيزُ ٱلْحَكِيمُ ﴾ (سورة المَائدة : ١١٨)

﴾If You punish them, they are Your slaves, and if You forgive them,
verily You, only You are the All-Mighty, the All-Wise.﴿
(Qur'an 5: 118)

And he (ﷺ) cried for the better part of what was left of that night.

It is authentically related that the Prophet (ﷺ) once said to
Ibn Mas'ood (ﷺ): "Recite the Qur'an to me." Ibn Mas'ood

replied, "How can I recite it to you, when upon you it was revealed?" The Prophet (ﷺ) replied, "Recite, for indeed, I would love to hear it from someone other than myself." Ibn Mas'ood proceeded to recite from the beginning of chapter *an-Nisâ'* until he reached the saying of Allah (ﷻ):

﴿فَكَيْفَ إِذَا جِئْنَا مِن كُلِّ أُمَّةٍ بِشَهِيدٍ وَجِئْنَا بِكَ عَلَىٰ هَٰؤُلَاءِ شَهِيدًا ۝﴾

(سورة النِّسَاء: ٤١)

❲How [will it be] then, when We bring from each nation a witness and We bring you [O Muhammad] as a witness against these people?❳
(Qur'an 4: 41)

When Ibn Mas'ood finished reciting this verse, the Prophet (ﷺ) said, "For the moment, that is enough for you." Recounting what happened next, Ibn Mas'ood later said, "I then looked up, and I saw that tears were flowing from his eyes."[70]

On another occasion, upon waking up in the middle of the night, the Prophet (ﷺ) heard Abu Moosa al-Ash'ari (ﷺ) recite the Qur'an. The following morning, the Prophet (ﷺ) said to Abu Moosa: "Would that you saw me while I was listening to your recitation; indeed, you have been given a flute from the flutes of the family of Dâwood."[71] Abu Moosa then said, "Had I known that you were listening to me, I would have tried to make my recitation beautiful for you."[72]

---

[70] Related by Bukhari (4582, 5055) and Muslim (800), on the authority of 'Abdullâh ibn Mas'ood.

[71] Related by Bukhari (5048) and Muslim (793), on the authority of Abu Moosa.

[72] While not being mentioned in either Bukhari's or Muslim's narration of the hadith, this added phrase is mentioned in Bayhaqi's narration of the hadith in=

In an authentic hadith, 'Abdullâh ibn ash-Shukhayr (ﷺ) said: "I once entered the place of Messenger of Allah (ﷺ) while he was praying, and I could clearly hear a wheezing sound emanating from his chest. That sound was him crying, and it was very similar to the sound of a pot (when the water inside of it begins to boil)."

At the funeral of his daughter Zaynab (ﷺ), the Prophet (ﷺ) sat by her grave, and all the while his eyes were flowing with tears. He cried as he contemplated death and that which comes after death — either an eternal life of bliss or an eternal life of torment in the Hellfire. And as he sat there crying, his Companions were moved by what they saw. They surely thought to themselves that, if the Prophet (ﷺ) — whose past and future sins were forgiven — was crying, surely they had even more reason to cry.

The Prophet (ﷺ) informed us of the great virtue of crying out of the fear of Allah (ﷺ). For while enumerating the seven categories of people that Allah will provide with shade on the Day when there will be no shade save His shade, the Prophet (ﷺ) said: "(And a) man who, while being alone, remembers Allah, at which point tears then flow from his eyes."[73] It is authentically related that the Prophet (ﷺ) said: "There are two eyes that will never be touched by the Hellfire: The eye that, while trembling, cries from the fear of Allah; and the eye that stays awake throughout the night, guarding (Muslims) in the way of Allah."[74]

=al-Kubrâ (4484, 20841) and ash-Shu'ab (2604).

[73] Related by Bukhari (660, 1423, 6806) and Muslim (1031), on the authority of Abu Hurayrah.

[74] Related by Tirmidhi (1639) and by Bayhaqi, in ash-Shu'ab (796), on the authority of Ibn 'Abbâs.

The crying that is legislated in Islam is the crying that is a direct consequence of fearing Allah, of contemplating Allah's signs in the universe, of remembering the time when one will have to stand before one's Lord for judgment. In such instances, crying is one of the noblest of deeds that Allah's righteous slaves can perform. Crying is especially praiseworthy when one cries because one regrets having sinned, because one fears Allah's punishment, because one feels mercy and compassion for the grief-stricken, or because one has heard a moving reminder about the Hereafter. But it is not praiseworthy, or even acceptable, for one to cry over some worldly reason, that reason being either one getting what one doesn't want, or one not getting what one wants. The world and all of its treasures are trifling, insignificant things, and are not, therefore, worth crying about.

The Prophet (ﷺ) cried for all the right reasons — because he had certain knowledge about what is to happen in the Hereafter, because he loved Allah, and because he feared Allah. He never once cried for missing out on some worldly thing — for not marrying a specific woman, for not getting a worthwhile return on an investment, for not being able to buy a certain property. No, the world and its treasures were trifling things to the Prophet (ﷺ). If the Prophet (ﷺ) cried or became sad, he did so for the sake of Allah. If he smiled or laughed, he also did so in the obedience of Allah. In every thing he did, he was an ideal example for Muslims:

(سورة الأحزاب: ٢١) ﴿لَّقَدْ كَانَ لَكُمْ فِي رَسُولِ اللَّهِ أُسْوَةٌ حَسَنَةٌ ... ﴾

﴿Indeed in the Messenger of Allah [Muhammad] you have a good example to follow...﴾ *(Qur'an 33: 21)*

When an insincere person cries, others are not moved to feel for his sadness; on the contrary, they probably feel contempt for him, either thinking that he is only pretending to cry or that he is crying for some silly, unimportant reason. But because of his sincerity, the Prophet (ﷺ) had an altogether different effect on people when he cried. His crying penetrated the depths of his Companions' hearts, and his crying, moreover, was contagious. When he stood on the pulpit and spoke about the horrors of the Day of Resurrection, and when he cried as he spoke, his entire audience broke out into tears as well. Hearing the Prophet's sobbing, the Companions were not able to contain their emotions. Imagine yourself watching the Prophet (ﷺ) and his Companions as they cried together not for some silly worldly reason, but because they all feared and loved Allah (ﷻ); because, together, they remembered some Religious teaching about the Hereafter; and because they were spiritually alive, unlike most of the people of this world.

People were moved by the Prophet's tears because his heart was filled with the fear of Allah and because his soul was overflowing with love for Allah. It was almost as if his tears were words that were being intelligibly conveyed to his followers, more eloquently, mind you, than virtually all of the speeches and sermons of other men. O Allah, send prayers and salutations on Muhammad, his family, and his Companions.

The Beautiful Laughter
of the Prophet

*M*oderate laughter is like a balm for the soul; it is comfort for a mind that is tired from hard work. It is a sign of a good-natured disposition; it is an indication of a balanced state of mind; and it is evidence of a pure and clean heart.

When the Messenger of Allah (ﷺ) would enter the place of his family, he would smile, he would laugh, and he would even joke around with his wives and other family members. He would bless them with his good company, his kind words, and his loving demeanor. Why should not that have been the case, for he was, after all, a mercy to all of mankind? The most deserving people of his good company and gracious demeanor were his family, his loved ones, and his Companions. And, to be sure, they were truly blessed, for whenever they met him, they had the good fortune to look upon a cheerful and smiling countenance. As a result of his cheerful demeanor and good manners, he captivated the souls of his Companions, who loved him with all of their hearts.

The Prophet (ﷺ) would joke, but even when he said something that was funny, he told the truth, never telling a lie in order to make others laugh. His smile, his good humour, his cheerful disposition — all of these, for the Companions, were like the gentle hand of a caring mother as it passed gently over the head of a beloved son. When the Prophet (ﷺ) would joke with his Companions, they would feel revitalized, with a new sense of vigor and energy in their souls. By Allah, in attending his gatherings, they had no worldly motives, no hidden agenda of gaining some worldly benefit. No, by Allah, in going to meet him, they hoped not to gain from him gold or silver or any other worldly treasure; instead, all that they desired was to be in his blessed company — that was enough for them, and that was all they wanted.

Jareer ibn 'Abdullâh al-Bajalee (راضی) said: "It never occurred that the Messenger of Allah (ﷺ) saw me without smiling at me." Jareer (راضی) was taking pride in the great gift that the Prophet (ﷺ) bestowed upon him — the gift of his love, compassion, and cheerfulness. For Jareer, a simple smile from the Prophet (ﷺ) was worth more than the world and all of its treasures, and more than any other good memory he could possibly have imagined. A simple smile from the Prophet (ﷺ) filled Jareer's soul — and the soul of any other Companion, for that matter — with peace and happiness. Do not think that I am overstating the matter; one would have had to be alive during that era to truly appreciate what it meant to be the recipient of the Prophet's smile and attention. Imagine that you were to meet a famous person or someone you regard highly, and then imagine how it would feel if that person were to actually speak to you, never mind simply greet you. Then imagine the happiness you would feel at that moment and how you would cherish that memory for the rest of your life. And that is the case regarding a common man. Now imagine receiving attention — and not just attention, but an actual loving smile — from the Messenger of the Lord of all that exists, and in so doing, you might better appreciate the above-mentioned saying of Jareer.

In his laughing, in his joking, and in his playing, the Prophet (ﷺ) was moderate, having struck a perfect balance between the extremes of a man who always has a frown on his face and a man who constantly laughs and jokes around without taking life seriously. The Prophet (ﷺ) would laugh when it was appropriate to laugh, just as he cried when it was appropriate to cry, or became angry when it was appropriate to be angry. One thing, however, is certain: he would not laugh immoderately, or to the point that his body would either shake or rock back and forth. It is authentically established that the Prophet (ﷺ) said: "Beware of laughing, for indeed frequent laughter kills the heart."[75] It is related in various narrations that the Prophet (ﷺ) would sometimes joke with his Companions. For instance, on one occasion, a man said to the Prophet (ﷺ): "O Messenger of Allah! I want you to give me a camel to ride upon." The Prophet said, "All that I can find for you is a child of a she-camel." The man turned around and walked away, disappointed that the Prophet (ﷺ) wanted to give him a baby camel upon which to ride. The Prophet (ﷺ) then called him back and said, "And is not every camel (be it old or young) the child of a she-camel!"[76]

On another occasion, an old woman went to the Prophet (ﷺ) and asked him to pray for her; she specifically wanted him to invoke Allah to grant her entry into Paradise. The Prophet (ﷺ) said: "No old woman enters Paradise." The woman, like the man from the previous example, walked away, but beyond being disappointed, she actually began to cry — and which man or woman would not cry upon being told that he or she could not enter Paradise? The Prophet (ﷺ) then called her back and said,

---

[75] Related by Aḥmad (8034), Tirmidhi (2305) and Ibn Mâjah (4217), on the authority of Abu Hurayrah. Refer to al-Bayân wat-Ta'reef (1/22) and Kashf al-Khifâ (85).

[76] Related by Aḥmad (13405), Abu Dâwood (4998) and Tirmidhi (1991), on the authority of Anas ibn Mâlik.

"Did you not hear the saying of Allah...?"[77] Having said this, the Prophet (ﷺ) then proceeded to recite the following verse, making it clear that, when a woman enters Paradise, she enters it as a young woman, even if, in this world, she died an old woman:

$$ ﴿ إِنَّآ أَنشَأْنَٰهُنَّ إِنشَآءً ۝ فَجَعَلْنَٰهُنَّ أَبْكَارًا ۝ عُرُبًا أَتْرَابًا ۝ ﴾ $$

(سورة الواقِعَة : ٣٥-٣٧)

❨Verily, We have created them [maidens] of special creation. And made them virgins. Loving [their husbands only], equal in age.❩

(Qur'an 56: 35-37)

When the Prophet (ﷺ) laughed, he did so in obedience to his Lord (ﷻ). He would not laugh frivolously or needlessly as a means of passing time — which is the way many of us laugh today. On one occasion, when the Prophet (ﷺ) mounted his riding animal, about to embark on a journey, he made the supplication of travelling; and then he said: "O Allah, forgive me my sin(s), for indeed, none can forgive sins except for You." Having said this, the Prophet (ﷺ) began to laugh. His Companions asked, "O Messenger of Allah, why are you laughing?" He said, "Your Lord laughs when (His) slave says, 'O Allah, forgive me my sins, for indeed, none can forgive sins except for You.' He (i.e., Allah) says, 'My slave knows that none forgives except Me (and yet he still utters that phrase).'"[78]

The Prophet (ﷺ) told his Companions the story of the last man to exit from the Hellfire. That man, upon exiting the Hellfire, will ask Allah (ﷻ), little by little, for more and more blessings. In

---

[77] Related by at-Ṭabarâni; refer to *Majmâ' az-Zawâid* (10/419).

[78] Related by Aḥmad (932), Abu Dâwood (2602), Tirmidhi (3446), on the authority of 'Ali. And Tirmidhi ruled that this hadith is authentic.

the end, the man will be made to understand that Allah will give him ten times more than he could have ever dreamed of himself. The man will then say to Allah, "Are You making fun of me (by making me think that I will get so much), and You are the Lord of all that exists?" When the Prophet (ﷺ) finished relating this saying, he began to laugh.

Allah (ﷻ) guided the Prophet (ﷺ) to always do what was right. As a result of that guidance, the Prophet (ﷺ) would always do what was befitting and proper considering the circumstances. During times of happiness and prosperity, and during leisure time, he would play and joke around in a moderate manner. During sermons and speeches, he would be serious in his demeanor, and he would cry out of the fear of Allah. The Prophet (ﷺ) was truly honored and blessed, for every smile he gave, every tear he shed, every joke he made, and every advice he gave is a part of his Sunnah. Every aspect of his life is related in books of hadith. A narrator might have travelled hundreds of miles to learn about a hadith which related a story of how the Prophet (ﷺ) smiled or cried or showed kindness to a little child. Even his laughter is recorded in books that are deemed sacred by Muslims worldwide. Then all glory be to Allah, Who has raised the ranking of His Messenger to such a high level that even his joking and laughing are related by one trustworthy narrator, from another trustworthy narrator, from another trustworthy narrator — as if that laugh is a compulsory deed that we must follow. O Allah, send prayers and salutations upon the Prophet, upon his family, and upon his Companions for as long as the sun rises in the morning and sets in the evening.

The Bravery of the Prophet

What the Prophet (ﷺ) might have lacked in terms of physical strength — and by all accounts, he certainly was strong — he more than amply made up for with bravery and fearlessness, qualities he possessed because he feared no one but Allah (ﷻ). In those days, battles were frightening affairs. Granted, war is always brutal, but in the Prophet's time soldiers did not fire bullets at one another from distances; instead, they physically clashed against one another, with swords raised; with heads flying in the air at the scene of the battle; with limbs being chopped off with powerful strokes of the sword; and with blood staining people's skin, clothing, and armor — not to mention pools of blood that formed in the ground. Just to voluntarily walk onto such a battlefield required a great deal of fortitude and courage. But the Prophet (ﷺ) did not just walk onto battlefields, standing safely behind rows of soldiers; on the contrary, he fought in the front row, quite often being nearer to the enemy than any other Muslim soldier.

The Prophet (ﷺ) never once fled from a battle; more telling, to be sure, is the fact that he never even retreated: If others defensively moved back a few feet or more when the enemy attacked, the Prophet (ﷺ) maintained his position, refusing to give up even an inch of ground to the enemy. At times, the Prophet (ﷺ) acted as a commander, supervising the proceedings of a battle from a command post. But when fighting intensified, when body parts flew into the air and blood sprayed out from exposed wounds, and when the decisive stages of battle were taking place

— the Prophet (ﷺ) was, without fail, at the forefront of his army, with calm nerves and with complete trust in his Lord.

In the early days of his migration to Madeenah, the Prophet (ﷺ) hid in a cave with Abu Bakr aṣ-Ṣiddeeq (ﷺ); neither of them was armed, and they were surrounded by polytheists who had unsheathed swords coupled with malevolent hearts, the most dangerous of combinations. These were men who wanted nothing more than to kill the Prophet (ﷺ). Upon seeing an expression of fear on Abu Bakr's face, the Prophet (ﷺ) said: "O Abu Bakr, what do you think of two (people), when Allah is the third (member) of their group."[79] That, without a doubt, is the pinnacle of bravery.

During the Battle of Ḥunayn, most Muslims fled from the battlefield during the initial stages of the battle. The only Muslims who remained steadfast on the battlefield were the Prophet (ﷺ) and six of his Companions. Mounted not even on a horse but instead on a riding mule, the Prophet (ﷺ) rode towards the members of the opposing army, who were many in number, and who were attired in armor virtually from head to toe. And yet the Prophet (ﷺ) continued to ride towards them, until finally, he took a handful of dirt in his hand and threw it into their direction, all the while saying, "May your faces turn ugly!"[80] By the Grace and Permission of Allah, the Almighty, All-Powerful, a miracle then occurred: pieces of that dirt entered the eyes of every single member of the opposing army, causing them all pain and discomfort. The tide of the battle then shifted in the favor of the Muslim army: Muslim soldiers returned to the battlefield, and

[79] Related by Bukhari (3653, 4663) and Muslim (2381), on the authority of Abu Bakr.
[80] Related by Muslim (1777), on the authority of Salamah ibn 'Amr ibn al-Akwa'.

shortly thereafter, Allah granted them a decisive victory over their enemies.

The praise the Prophet received

*I*n this section, we will discuss the various ways in which the Prophet (ﷺ) was praised. His very name, *Muhammad*, comprehensively describes who he was as a person. In Arabic, the name Muhammad conveys the meaning of *Mamdooh*, which means "to be praised". All of the qualities of the Prophet (ﷺ) were praiseworthy and commendable.

No sooner is the Prophet's name mentioned than one thinks of virtue, nobility, chastity, uprightness, and piety. Allah (ﷺ) said:

﴿ ... نَافِلَةً لَّكَ عَسَىٰٓ أَن يَبْعَثَكَ رَبُّكَ مَقَامًا مَّحْمُودًا ﴿٧٩﴾ ﴾ (سورة الإسرَاء: ٧٩)

﴿... It may be that your Lord may raise you up to *Maqâm Mahmood* [a station of praise and glory, i.e. the highest degree in Paradise!]﴾

(Qur'an: 17: 79)

Muhammad ibn 'Abdullâh: It is a name whose letters are inscribed with rays of light on the hearts of true believers. The Prophet (ﷺ) was praised in the Torah and the Injeel (the Gospel). The Messengers that came before him mentioned him to their people, and previously revealed scriptures contained glad tidings of his arrival on earth.

The Prophet (ﷺ) was protected from misguidance:

﴿مَا ضَلَّ صَاحِبُكُمْ وَمَا غَوَىٰ ۝﴾ (سورة النَّجْم : ٢)

﴿Your companion [Muhammad] has neither gone astray nor has he erred.﴾ *(Qur'an: 53: 2)*

He (ﷺ) was protected from following his desires:

﴿وَمَا يَنطِقُ عَنِ ٱلْهَوَىٰ ۝﴾ (سورة النَّجْم : ٣)

﴿Nor does he speak of [his own] desire.﴾ *(Qur'an 53: 3)*

His words were divine law, and his Sunnah was revelation from his Lord:

﴿إِنْ هُوَ إِلَّا وَحْىٌ يُوحَىٰ ۝﴾ (سورة النَّجْم : ٤)

﴿It is only a revelation revealed.﴾ *(Qur'an: 53: 4)*

He (ﷺ) was upright, following the truth in everything he did:

﴿فَتَوَكَّلْ عَلَى ٱللَّهِ إِنَّكَ عَلَى ٱلْحَقِّ ٱلْمُبِينِ ۝﴾ (سورة النَّمْل : ٧٩)

﴿So put your trust in Allah; surely you [O Muhammad] are on the manifest truth.﴾ *(Qur'an: 27: 79)*

He (ﷺ) was a paragon of humbleness, being noble in his manners, truthful in everything he said and did, and generous to an almost unbelievable degree:

﴿وَإِنَّكَ لَعَلَىٰ خُلُقٍ عَظِيمٍ ۝﴾ (سورة القَلَم : ٤)

﴿And verily, you [O Muhammad] are on an exalted [standard of] character.﴾ *(Qur'an: 68: 4)*

He was gentle and easy-going, and not harsh or stern:

﴿فَبِمَا رَحْمَةٍ مِّنَ اللَّهِ لِنتَ لَهُمْ وَلَوْ كُنتَ فَظًّا غَلِيظَ الْقَلْبِ لَانفَضُّوا مِنْ حَوْلِكَ فَاعْفُ عَنْهُمْ وَاسْتَغْفِرْ لَهُمْ وَشَاوِرْهُمْ فِي الْأَمْرِ فَإِذَا عَزَمْتَ فَتَوَكَّلْ عَلَى اللَّهِ إِنَّ اللَّهَ يُحِبُّ الْمُتَوَكِّلِينَ ﴿١٥٩﴾﴾

(سورة آل عِمرَان: ١٥٩)

﴾And by the Mercy of Allah you dealt with them gently. And had you been severe and harsh-hearted, they would have broken away from about you; so pass over [their faults], and ask [Allah's] Forgiveness for them; and consult them in the affairs. Then when you have taken a decision, put your trust in Allah, certainly, Allah loves those who put their trust [in Him].﴾ *(Qur'an: 3: 159)*

The Prophet (ﷺ) was noble himself, and what made him even more extraordinary was the fact that he was surrounded from all directions by Allah's divine care, protection, and help:

﴿إِنَّا فَتَحْنَا لَكَ فَتْحًا مُّبِينًا ﴿١﴾﴾

(سورة الفَتْح: ١)

﴾Verily, We have given you [O Muhammad] a manifest victory.﴾ *(Qur'an: 48: 1)*

Beyond being protected by Allah (ﷻ), he was forgiven for all of his past and future sins:

﴿لِيَغْفِرَ لَكَ اللَّهُ مَا تَقَدَّمَ مِن ذَنبِكَ وَمَا تَأَخَّرَ ...﴾

(سورة الفَتْح: ٢)

﴾That Allah may forgive you your sins of the past and the future...﴾ *(Qur'an: 48: 2)*

And why should he not have been praised? He was, after all, one who was sent to purify the hearts of people; to bring happiness to all human beings; to save mankind from the shackles of slavery to all created beings; and to bring true freedom to all human beings, making them slaves to no one save Allah (ﷻ).

❨And verily, you [O Muhammad] are indeed guiding [mankind] to the Straight Path [i.e. Allah's religion of Islamic Monotheism].❩

(Qur'an: 42: 52)

He (ﷺ) came to make matters easy for people, to present to them a Religion whose teachings are easy to follow:

﴿ ... وَيَضَعُ عَنْهُمْ إِصْرَهُمْ وَٱلْأَغْلَٰلَ ٱلَّتِى كَانَتْ عَلَيْهِمْ ... ﴿١٥٧﴾ ﴾

(سورة الأعراف: ١٥٧)

❨... He releases them from their heavy burdens [of Allah's Covenant], and from the fetters [bindings] that were upon them...❩

(Qur'an: 7: 157)

The Messenger of Allah (ﷺ) was a mercy to mankind — and why wouldn't he have been when he himself had been taught by the Most Merciful of the merciful ones?

The Prophet (ﷺ) was a mercy for old people, instructing them to do acts of worship that were easy and not difficult; thus he did not place upon them a burden that was greater than they were able to bear. He exhorted them to make good use of their final years and advised them to strive to make the last of their deeds the best of their deeds.

The Prophet (ﷺ) was a mercy to young people, inculcating them with a set of lofty manners, exhorting them to make good use of their youth, and giving them kind words of encouragement — something that all young people need.

He (ﷺ) was a mercy to babies, showering them with his love and compassion, blessing them with the sound of the *Adhân* (the call to Prayer) immediately following their exit from their mothers' wombs, and advising their parents to give them good names.

He (ﷺ) was a mercy to women, being just to them amid a world that was filled with injustice, giving them all of their intrinsic rights, safeguarding their honor, and bestowing upon them the honor and dignity they deserved as human beings.

He (ﷺ) was a mercy to leaders, rulers, and governors, establishing for them a comprehensive political system that is based on justice and mercy; warning them not to become corrupt or ruthless; and teaching them how, through kindness and good deeds and compassion, to gain the love and respect of common citizens.

He (ﷺ) was a mercy to common citizens, defending their rights, forbidding any form of transgression against them, and ordering them to obey their leaders so long as their leaders did not command them to disobey Allah (ﷻ), a command that was meant for their benefit — to keep their Nation strong and united. The Messenger of Allah (ﷺ) was a mercy and a blessing for everyone:

﴿وَمَآ أَرْسَلْنَٰكَ إِلَّا رَحْمَةً لِّلْعَٰلَمِينَ ۝﴾   (سورة الأنبياء: ١٠٧)

❪And We have sent you [O Muhammad] not but as a mercy for the 'Âlameen [mankind, jinns, and all that exists].❫   *(Qur'an 21: 107)*

It is often said that, when an insincere man speaks, his words barely enter the ears of his audience; and that, when a sincere person speaks, his words enter his audience's ears, making it all the way to their hearts. Imagine, then, the effect that the Prophet's words had on the Companions. Without a doubt, his words penetrated the deepest regions of their hearts, becoming permanently etched in the Companions' memories and souls. When he (ﷺ) spoke, the Companions bowed their heads with attentiveness, not moving a single millimeter, as if they felt that birds were perched on their heads, and they didn't want them to fly away.

Such was the effect of the Prophet's speech during normal conversation. When he delivered sermons, it was as if the pulpit beneath him shook. The hearts of his listeners sprang into a state of attentive wakefulness; each person present entered into a state of spiritual rapture, exiting — at least mentally and spiritually — from the mundaneness of this life, and soaring into the realm of the Hereafter. Had a stone attended the Prophet's sermons, it too would have been moved to tears; had a wall been an audience member, it too would have trembled from the fear of Allah; and if the days had ears, they too would have silently and attentively listened to the Prophet's words. When the Prophet (ﷺ) delivered a sermon, it was as if the Companions felt that the angel of death was swooping down to take them away, which is why, if one were to look down upon their gatherings, one would not find a single dry eye.

﴿أَفَمِنْ هَٰذَا ٱلْحَدِيثِ تَعْجَبُونَ ۝ وَتَضْحَكُونَ وَلَا تَبْكُونَ ۝﴾ (سورة النَّجم: ٥٩-٦٠)

﴿Do you then wonder about this recitation [the Qur'an]? And you laugh at it and weep not.﴾　　　　　　　　　　*(Qur'an 53: 59, 60)*

When he fought, he was as firm as a mountain, and he advanced forward towards the enemy with the unrelenting resolve and fierceness of a flood.

﴿فَقَٰتِلْ فِى سَبِيلِ ٱللَّهِ لَا تُكَلَّفُ إِلَّا نَفْسَكَ ... ۝﴾　　(سورة النِّساء: ٨٤)

﴿Then fight [O Muhammad] in the Cause of Allah, you are not tasked [held responsible] except for yourself...﴾　　　　*(Qur'an 4: 84)*

The worse a situation became during a battle, the braver the Prophet (ﷺ) became. And he fought with a strong appreciation of the fact that death was written for him and that he would not die until the moment during which Allah (ﷻ) decreed for him to die:

﴿وَمَا مُحَمَّدٌ إِلَّا رَسُولٌ قَدْ خَلَتْ مِن قَبْلِهِ الرُّسُلُ أَفَإِين مَّاتَ أَوْ قُتِلَ انقَلَبْتُمْ عَلَىٰ أَعْقَـٰبِكُمْ وَمَن يَنقَلِبْ عَلَىٰ عَقِبَيْهِ فَلَن يَضُرَّ اللَّهَ شَيْئًا وَسَيَجْزِى اللَّهُ الشَّـٰكِرِينَ ﴾

(سورة آل عِمرَان: ١٤٤)

﴿Muhammad is no more than a Messenger, and indeed [many] Messengers have passed away before him. If he dies or is killed, will you then turn back on your heels [as disbelievers]? And he who turns back on his heels, not the least harm will he do to Allah; and Allah will give reward to those who are grateful.﴾ *(Qur'an: 3: 144)*

When it came to the quality of generosity, no one surpassed the Prophet (ﷺ) — no one could have done so back then, and no one can do so today. The simple reality is that all people, at least to a certain degree, keep money with them because they are afraid that they will need it at some point in the future. As for the Prophet (ﷺ), he did not fear poverty, and he was not afraid of the future; instead, he had complete trust in the fact that Allah would provide for him. The Prophet (ﷺ) was generous in every possible way: He was generous with his time, dedicating it all to the cause of Islam; he was generous with his wealth, giving it away, often leaving little or nothing for himself; and he was even generous with his life, fighting in the front lines of battle, always willing to give up his life for the sake of Allah.

The wealth he owned he was willing to give away in an instant. On certain occasions, he gave hundreds of camels away as gifts to various Arab chieftains. He once said: "If I had wealth that was equal in quantity to the trees of *Tihâmah* (i.e., a very large sum of wealth), I would have distributed it, and you would not have found me to be a miser, a liar, or a coward (regarding the manner in which I would liberally give away all of that wealth)."

Once, when asked for the very shirt on his back, the Prophet (ﷺ) did not hesitate to remove it and give it to the man who asked for it. Ḥâtim was generous because he wanted fame and popularity; the Prophet (ﷺ), on the other hand, was generous for the sake of Allah.

The Prophet's generosity had a profound effect on others. He forgave people their transgressions against him, without reproaching them and without seeking retribution. This had the effect of winning over the hearts and minds of the staunchest of his enemies.

(سورة الحِجر: ٨٥) ﴿ ... فَٱصۡفَحِ ٱلصَّفۡحَ ٱلۡجَمِيلَ ﴾

❨... So overlook [O Muhammad], their faults with gracious forgiveness. [This was before the ordainment of *Jihad* — holy fighting in Allah's cause].❩ *(Qur'an: 15: 85)*

After a group of fellow tribesmen rejected his message, called him a 'liar' and a 'magician', persecuted him for a number of years, forced him to leave his homeland, and then waged war against him for another long period of time — after all of that, the Prophet (ﷺ) forgave them, saying to them on the day of the Conquest of Makkah, "Go (forth in safety), for you are the freed ones."

And he (ﷺ) summarized his generous attitude towards others with his saying: "Verily, Allah ordered me to keep relations with those that cut me off, to forgive the one who does an injustice to me, and to give to those who withhold from me."[81]

Every noble characteristic that is described in the Qur'an the Prophet (ﷺ) translated into real-life application. It is for this reason that 'Â'ishah (ﺭﺿﻲ) said about him: "His character was the Qur'an."

When the Prophet (ﷺ) made a promise, he always fulfilled it. His enemies could not remember a single instance in which he broke his promise or reneged on the terms of an agreement. They desired nothing more than to find a single fault of his, a single mistake to blemish his reputation; but in spite of all their efforts, they could find not a single mistake, not a single slip-up, not a single indiscretion. Throughout his life — whether in times of peace or in times of war, whether he was happy or angry, whether he was troubled with some matter or safe and calm — he remained consistently truthful and trustworthy. A man once made an appointment to meet him at a certain place. The Prophet (ﷺ) then not only kept his appointment, but when the man did not show up, he waited for him for three days, fearing that, if he left, the man might show up at any time and not find him there — such was the extent of the Prophet's trustworthiness. He signed treaties with polytheists and Jews, and even though those two groups of people dedicated their lives to waging war against him, he never once violated the terms of the treaties he signed with them, and he never once broke a promise that he made to them. It was only natural for him to be trustworthy and faithful, for he came with a just, fair, and truthful set of laws (Shari'ah). The Prophet (ﷺ) warned against lying, breaking promises, and acting treacherously regarding the agreements one makes with others. He (ﷺ) said:

---

[81] Related by Razeen. Refer to *al-Mishkât al-Maṣâbeeḥ* (5358) and to *Tafseer al-Qurṭubi* (7/346).

"The signs of a hypocrite are three: when he speaks, he lies; when he promises, he breaks his promise; when he is trusted, he betrays his trust."[82]

And upon the Prophet (ﷺ) the following verses were revealed:

(سورة الإسراء: ٣٤)   ﴿ ... وَأَوْفُوا بِٱلْعَهْدِ إِنَّ ٱلْعَهْدَ كَانَ مَسْئُولًا ۝ ﴾

◀... And fulfill [every] covenant. Verily, the covenant, will be questioned about.▶   *(Qur'an: 17: 34)*

(سورة الرّعد: ٢٠)   ﴿ ٱلَّذِينَ يُوفُونَ بِعَهْدِ ٱللَّهِ وَلَا يَنقُضُونَ ٱلْمِيثَٰقَ ۝ ﴾

◀Those who fulfill the Covenant of Allah and break not the *Mithâq* [bond, treaty, covenant].▶   *(Qur'an 13: 20)*

The Prophet as an orator

(سورة النِّسَاء: ٦٣)   ﴿ ... وَعِظْهُمْ وَقُل لَّهُمْ فِىٓ أَنفُسِهِمْ قَوْلًۢا بَلِيغًا ۝ ﴾

◀... But admonish them, and speak to them an effective word [i.e., to believe in Allah, worship Him, obey Him, and be afraid of Him] to reach their innerselves.▶   *(Qur'an 4: 63)*

If one were to read the various sayings of the Prophet (ﷺ), one would be amazed by his eloquence. His speech, by Allah,

---

[82] Related by Bukhari (33/2682) and Muslim (59), on the authority of Abu Hurayrah.

had, and continues to have, the effect of captivating the souls of people. Brilliantly crafted sentences, well-chosen words, compact and cohesive phrases, succinctness coupled with fluency — all of these were the trademarks of the Prophet's speech. In short, his speech was pithy: He (ﷺ) always spoke briefly, but everything he said conveyed profound meanings. He said about himself: "I have been given the most comprehensive of phrases."[83] According to one particular narration, the Prophet (ﷺ) said: "I have been blessed with very pithy speech."[84]

Even though the Prophet (ﷺ) was very succinct in his speech — and the *Ahâdeeth* that contain his actual sayings are approximately ten thousand in number — his various sayings comprehensively cover all areas of this life, of life in the Hereafter, of news about the past, and of news about what is to come in the future. If you want to gain a better appreciation of the true eloquence and beauty of the Prophet's speech, then compare it to the speech of any other human being — especially to the sayings of the greatest of poets, the most famous of orators, or the most celebrated of writers. Were you to peruse any book of quotations, any book that contains sayings of great and eloquent men, you would find the Prophet's sayings to be more eloquent and beautiful than anything that that book contains. In fact, if you were to compare the Prophet's speech with that of other eloquent people, you would find their sayings to be stilted at worse, and average at best.

---

[83] Related by Bukhari (2977) and Muslim (523). The above-mentioned wording of the hadith is taken from Imam Muslim's narration, which is related on the authority of Abu Hurayrah.

[84] Related by al-Bayhaqi in *ash-Shu'ab* (1436), on the authority of 'Umar. Refer also to *Kashf al-Khifâ* (1/14, 15).

An illiterate man who has never before read a book or studied literature, a student of knowledge, a teacher, an eloquent poet, a seasoned student of literature — if you were to gather all of these people and read to them some of the sayings of the Prophet (ﷺ), each one of them would equally be captivated and amazed by the superior eloquence of the Messenger of Allah (ﷺ).

One day, when the Prophet (ﷺ) intended to give Mu'âdh ibn Jabal (رضي الله عنه) some beneficial advice, he wanted to impart to him words that were at once brief and yet comprehensive in their meanings. And so he said to him, "Wherever you are, fear Allah, and follow a bad deed with a good deed, and the latter will erase the former; and in dealing with people, treat them with good and kind manners."[85] Had any other person, no matter how eloquent he is deemed, desired to impart advice that was similarly comprehensive and full of meaning, he would likely speak for many minutes, if not hours. He would either achieve meaning at the expense of brevity, whereby he would speak for a long period of time and confuse — and perhaps even bore — his audience; or he would achieve brevity at the expense of meaning, whereby he would be brief without doing justice to the topic.

'Uqbah ibn 'Âmir (رضي الله عنه) related that he once said: "O Messenger of Allah, what is safety (i.e., how does one achieve safety)?" The Prophet (ﷺ) answered, "Hold back your tongue, let your house be sufficient for you, and cry over your sin(s)."[86] To be sure, this succinct advice contains profound meanings that any

---

[85] Related by Aḥmad (20847, 20894), Tirmidhi (1987), and ad-Dârimi (2791). Refer also to al-Mishkât al-Maṣâbeeḥ (5083).

[86] Related by Aḥmad (21732); Tirmidhi (2406); and by Ibn Abi 'Âṣim, in az-Zuhd (1/15). Having related this hadith on the authority of 'Uqbah ibn 'Âmir, Ibn Abi 'Âṣim ruled it to be authentic.

other person could convey — if he could convey it at all — only with a lengthy speech, and yet the truly amazing thing is that the Prophet (ﷺ) gave his pithy answer without any prior preparation, without having taken notes beforehand. He had no chance to prepare an answer, for the questioner was standing right in front of him, eagerly waiting for his response.

In fact, that was precisely the most incredible aspect of all of the Prophet's sayings: Everything he said was unrehearsed, extemporaneous. Even the best of orators need, if not cue cards, then at least some form of rehearsal or preparation or planning. No one can just stand before a group of people and extemporaneously give a flawless, pithy, comprehensive speech. But that is precisely what the Prophet (ﷺ) did day in and day out — which should not come as a surprise, for his sayings were a form of divine revelation. Consider the advice he once gave Ibn 'Abbâs (رضي الله عنه). The two of them were riding together when, suddenly, the Prophet (ﷺ) said to Ibn 'Abbâs: "O young boy, I will teach you some phrases: Preserve Allah (i.e., preserve His rights, by obeying His commands and staying away from matters that He prohibited), and He will then preserve you (by keeping you safe in this world and in the Hereafter). Preserve Allah, and you will then find Him before you. Get to know Allah in times of ease, and He will know you (care for you, protect you, provide for you) in times of hardship. When you ask, ask Allah. And when you seek help, seek help from Allah. And know that, if the Nation were to gather in order to benefit you with something, they would not benefit you except with what Allah has written for you. And were (the Nation) to gather in order to harm you with something, they would not harm you except with what Allah has written for you. The pens have been raised, and the scrolls have dried. And know that victory comes with patience, that with hardship there is a way out, and that with difficulty comes ease."[87]

On paper, how very few lines of space this saying requires! And yet how profound and deep are its meanings! Have you ever come across any human speech that is similar to this? The phrasing is flawless, the meanings are powerful, and the overall effect is captivating. What the Prophet (ﷺ) said in this hadith was brief enough to memorize easily, and yet was comprehensive enough to benefit a person in all aspects of his life. How many problems in life would we be able to solve, how many sins would we be able to avoid, and how many adversities would we be able to overcome if we were to constantly remember that most succinct of reminders, "Preserve Allah, and He will then preserve you"? It is impossible to put that advice more succinctly, and the same holds true for the remainder of the hadith (mind you, only in the original Arabic can the superior eloquence of the hadith be truly appreciated).

Take any other of the many recorded sayings of the Prophet (ﷺ), and you will be similarly amazed by the Prophet's eloquence. In those sayings, you will not find a single word out of place, not a single word that could be replaced by a better word, not a single instance of a stilted, affected, or tritely-expressed sentence. Instead, his sayings were always straightforward yet expressive, brief yet full of meaning, simple yet graceful. Certain eminent scholars from the past would recognize a fabricated hadith narration not based on a defect in the chain of narrators, but on the weak diction of the actual hadith. They had read so many

---

[87] Related by Aḥmad (2664, 2758, 2800), Tirmidhi (2516), and al-Ḥākim (6304), on the authority of Ibn 'Abbâs. Refer to *al-Mishkât al-Maṣâbeeḥ* (5302).

thousands of *Aḥâdeeth*, and had thus become so accustomed to the unfailing eloquence of the Prophet (ﷺ), that a weak sentence was a clear indication that the narration could not possibly be ascribed to the Prophet (ﷺ).

In a hadith that is related by 'Umar ibn al-Khaṭṭâb (ﷺ), the Prophet (ﷺ) said: "Verily, deeds are only by their intentions, and for every person is only that which he intends."[88] This succinct saying has become more than a simple maxim; it is a fundamental and binding principle that covers all aspects of Islamic teachings — beliefs, manners, laws, and jurisprudence. In spite of its brevity, it is such a powerful saying that it has become a governing principle for scholars, a precept for the wise, and an oft-quoted aphorism for poets and writers.

During times of sadness, the Prophet (ﷺ) had the gift of saying something that was at once beautiful and comforting, something that quickly relieved the tension a bereaved or grief-stricken person was feeling. And in certain situations, the Prophet (Blessings and peace be upon him) would use wit, or more specifically a humorous play on words, to make someone feel better. Anas (may Allah be pleased with him) said: "Of all people, the Prophet (Blessings and peace be upon him) had the best manners. I had a brother whose name was Abu 'Umayr. When the Prophet (ﷺ) once came (to us) — I think that, at the time, Abu 'Umayr was just a newly-weaned child — and said, 'O Abu 'Umayr, what has the *Nughayr* done?' The word *Nughayr*, which means a small bird, rhymed with the child's name, Abu 'Umayr. The Prophet (ﷺ) eloquently used this rhyming play on words in

---

[88] Related by Bukhari (1, 54) and Muslim (1907), on the authority of 'Umar ibn al-Khaṭṭâb.

order to cheer up Abu 'Umayr, who was sad because the small bird that he used to play with had just died.[89]

It should come as no surprise that the Prophet (ﷺ) was the most eloquent of people; after all, the greatest miracle he came with was the Qur'an, which, in its perfection, grandeur, and magnificence, amazed the most eloquent of Arabs.

The Prophet as a legal jurist

Allah (ﷻ) said:

﴿وَيَسْتَفْتُونَكَ فِي ٱلنِّسَآءِ قُلِ ٱللَّهُ يُفْتِيكُمْ فِيهِنَّ ... ۝﴾

(سورة النِّساء: ١٢٧)

﴿They ask your legal instruction concerning women, say: Allah instructs you about them...﴾ *(Qur'an 4: 127)*

Not every knowledgeable person has the right to issue legal rulings. To be a jurist or judge requires a special set of qualities and talents; knowledge is one quality that is needed, but it is not the only one. A jurist or judge needs wisdom, foresight, a nuanced understanding, an appreciation of a questioner's situation, the ability to lend each situation its due level of importance, and so on. As for the Prophet (ﷺ), Allah blessed him when it came to

---

[89] Related by Bukhari (6129, 6203) and Muslim (2150), on the authority of Anas ibn Mâlik.

issuing legal rulings, bestowing upon him knowledge, understanding, wisdom, and many other relevant noble qualities besides. When various people came to him with a similar question or request — such as: "Advise me, O Messenger of Allah" — he would not repeat the same answer for each questioner; rather, he would, in each instance, give an answer that was appropriate to the questioner's circumstances — an answer that would benefit the questioner both in this life and in the Hereafter.

Whenever a person would come to the Prophet (ﷺ) with a question, it was as if the Prophet had already read that person's entire biography, having gained an intimate knowledge of that person's background, way of thinking, and personal circumstances. This was a direct result of the blessedness of revelation and of being guided by Allah (ﷻ).

The Prophet (ﷺ) would give each questioner an answer that was a solution to the most serious of his problems, or an answer that showed him the best way to become a better Muslim; or in other words, the Prophet (ﷺ) gave him the advice he most desperately needed.

An ailing elderly man went to the Prophet (ﷺ) and asked him to advise him. Because he was weak and frail, the old man could no longer stand up and pray for long periods of time; he was not able to fast; he was not able to endure the hardships of a journey, and so performing Ḥajj was out of the question. He therefore wanted to learn some simple and easy deed he could perform, a deed that required little physical effort on the one hand, and that entailed great rewards on the other. He did not explain all of this in his question, but the Prophet (ﷺ) understood well enough his circumstances. And so the Prophet (ﷺ) said: "Let your tongue remain moist with the remembrance of Allah."[90]

Here, the Prophet (ﷺ) told him to do something that did not require him to exercise his limbs, to walk long distances, or to lift heavy weights; instead, the deed he told him to perform involved — at least on a physical level — nothing more than moving his tongue. And not only was the actual deed simple, but the words the Prophet (ﷺ) used to describe the deed were also simple, eloquent, and easy to memorize. Had the old man gone to someone else with the very same question, that person would likely have advised him to take advantage of his final years by doing a great many deeds — deeds that the old man, given his frail condition, certainly would not have been able to perform.

Such was the easy-to-follow advice the Prophet (ﷺ) gave to an old and frail man. Now consider what the Prophet (ﷺ) said when a strong, well-built, and muscular man went to the Prophet (ﷺ) and asked for his advice. That man was Ghaylân ath-Thaqafi (رضي الله عنه), and he asked the Prophet (ﷺ) to guide him to a deed that would bring him closer to Allah. As with the example of the old man, the Prophet (ﷺ) responded with a succinct, simple, and easy-to-memorize answer; but unlike the example that involved the old man, the Prophet (ﷺ) replied by giving the physically-strong Ghaylân advice that was difficult to follow — which was appropriate considering Ghaylân's ability to meet a tough challenge. The Prophet (ﷺ) said to him: "Perform Jihad in the way of Allah." So because Ghaylân (رضي الله عنه) was endowed with both strength and energy, the Prophet (ﷺ) told him to join the Muslim army and to participate in battles against Islam's enemies.

---

[90] Related by Aḥmad (17227, 17245), Tirmidhi (3375) and Ibn Mâjah (3793); refer to al-Mishkât al-Maṣâbeeḥ (2279).

On another occasion, Abu Dharr (﷽) asked the Prophet (﷽) to advise him. Did the Prophet (﷽) tell him to "keep his tongue moist with the remembrance of Allah" or to "perform Jihad in the way of Allah"? No, he didn't. Both remembering Allah and performing Jihad are commendable deeds, but the way Abu Dharr asked his question indicated that he wanted advice regarding just one important matter. And so because of Abu Dharr's circumstances — namely, the fact that, on a personal level, he had anger-management issues to deal with — the Prophet (﷽) repeated the following advice three times: "Do not become angry."[91] This was just the cure that Abu Dharr needed; it was the very advice that, if applied, would make his life, and the life of others around him, much easier. Furthermore, that seemingly simple and yet profoundly important advice — "do not become angry" — was helpful not just to Abu Dharr, but also to many others, for it became a fundamental principle of Islamic Law.

And upon once seeing Abu Moosa al-Ash'ari (﷽) climbing a mountain, the Prophet (﷽) said: "Say, 'There is neither might nor power except with Allah', for indeed, it (i.e., this phrase) is a treasure from the treasures of Paradise."[92] Why was this advice appropriate to Abu Moosa's situation? Abu Moosa was climbing a mountain, an endeavor that requires strength and effort, an endeavor that can only be accomplished through Allah's help. And so one is likely to be helped by Allah in that endeavor when one humbly acknowledges one's own weakness, and when one acknowledges the fact that "there is neither might nor power except with Allah".

---

[91] Related by Bukhari (6116), on the authority of Abu Hurayrah.

[92] Related by Bukhari (4205, 6610) and Muslim (2704), on the authority of Abu Moosa.

The Prophet (ﷺ) was blessed when it came to assessing people's talents and abilities. To each person he assigned tasks that were in keeping with that person's qualifications and talents. And so, for instance, because Ḥassân (ﷺ) was an eloquent poet, the Prophet (ﷺ) would ask him to compose verses of poetry that promoted the cause of Islam; but he did not ask Ḥassân to judge between people in their disputes, because among the Prophet's Companions, Ḥassân was not known to be an eminent or knowledgeable jurist. If a Companion was knowledgeable and wise, the Prophet (ﷺ) would ask him to judge people's disputes; if a man was strong, physically well-built, and energetic, the Prophet (ﷺ) would ask him to become a soldier in the Muslim army; if a man possessed good leadership qualities, the Prophet (ﷺ) would appoint him to be one of his governors in a distant province; and if a man was knowledgeable and possessed good manners, the Prophet (ﷺ) would ask him to teach others about Islam — as happened in the case of Mus'ab ibn 'Umayr (ﷺ) when the Prophet (ﷺ) sent him to Madeenah to teach the native inhabitants of of that city about Islam. Just as the Prophet (ﷺ) employed people based on their talents and abilities, he warned certain people not to overstep the bounds of their talents and enter a field of work for which they were neither suited nor qualified. For instance, the Prophet (ﷺ) knew that Abu Dharr (ﷺ) was good at certain things but that he was not suited for leadership positions. Perhaps the Prophet (ﷺ) recognized in Abu Dharr a lack of patience and a lack of certain other qualities that every good leader must possess. And so the Prophet (ﷺ) advised Abu Dharr not to take on leadership positions. The Prophet (ﷺ) cared deeply for Abu Dharr, not wanting him to be in a position in which he would not be able to fulfill his duties as a leader, which would result in him having to carry a heavy burden on the Day of

Resurrection. After all, in Islam, to be a leader is not as much a privilege as it is a great responsibility, one for which a leader will be held accountable for on the Day of Resurrection. Contemplate, then, the deep understanding that the Prophet (ﷺ) had about the talents and abilities of people:

﴾إِنْ هُوَ إِلَّا وَحْيٌ يُوحَى ۝﴿   (سورة النّجم: ٤)

﴾It is only a revelation revealed.﴿   *(Qur'an: 53: 4)*

And when the Prophet (ﷺ) sent Mu'âdh (﵁) to Yemen, he said to him: "Verily, you are going to a people from the People of the Book (i.e. either Jews or Christians)."[93] The Prophet (ﷺ) said this so that Mu'âdh would know the situation of the people to whom he was going, and so that he could advise them in an appropriate manner, a manner that suited their circumstances.

And while they were riding a donkey together, the Prophet (ﷺ) advised Mu'âdh, telling him about rights that Allah has over his slaves and rights that they have over Allah. On this occasion, the Prophet (ﷺ) provided detailed information because Mu'âdh was not just a scholar, but also a man who was going on a mission to invite others to Islam. He was at once a teacher, a guide, and a judge. Had the Prophet been riding with someone else — say a Bedouin, for instance — the same detailed advice would not have been as appropriate, and, to be sure, the Prophet (ﷺ) would have given that other person simple advice that was suitable to his situation.

On one occasion, when Ḥusayn ibn 'Ubayd went to him, the Prophet (ﷺ) asked: "How many (gods) do you worship?"

---

[93] Related by Bukhari (1458, 1496) and Muslim (19), on the authority Ibn 'Abbâs.

Ḥusayn answered, "I worship seven: six on the earth and one in the heavens." The Prophet (ﷺ) asked, "Which of them do you hope from and fear?" He replied, "The One in the heavens." The Prophet (ﷺ) said, "Then abandon the ones on the earth and worship the One in the heavens." The Prophet (ﷺ) then said to him, "Say, 'O Allah, inspire me to right guidance and protect me from the evil of my own self.'"[94] This supplication was appropriate for the situation of Ḥusayn ibn 'Ubayd, considering his confused state of mind and considering how far away he was from the truth. Thus it was most befitting for the Prophet (ﷺ) to teach Ḥusayn two things: to ask Allah (ﷻ) for guidance and to seek refuge from the evil of his own self.

And the following is the advice that the Prophet (ﷺ) gave to 'Ali ibn Abi Ṭâlib (ﷺ): "Say, 'O Allah, guide me and direct me (to the right path).'"[95] This supplication was appropriate considering 'Ali's circumstances. 'Ali was to outlive many of the Prophet's Companions, and he would be alive during an era of great trials and tribulations, an era during which the truth would remain concealed from many men; thus it was important for him to learn a supplication in which he asked Allah (ﷻ) for guidance, so that when those difficult times came, he could clearly see through clouds of darkness and know the light of truth.

Then glory be to Allah, Who guided His Messenger and blessed him with the ability to give each person advice that was appropriate to his situation and circumstances.

---

[94] Related by Tirmidhi (3483), Lâlkâee (1184), on the authority of 'Imrân ibn Ḥusayn; refer to al-Mishkât al-Maṣâbeeḥ (2476).

[95] Related by Muslim (2725), on the authority of 'Ali ibn Abi Ṭâlib.

The Prophet (ﷺ) did not talk like poets, who are known to speak frequently about that which they have no knowledge, and who are known to wander aimlessly from one valley of thought to another. Led by their imagination and their fancy, poets seemingly say much but in reality say very little. As for the Prophet (ﷺ), Allah (ﷻ) protected him from vain and pompous speech, blessing him instead with speech that was a form of revelation. And the Prophet (ﷺ) did not speak in the affected manner of politicians, a group of people who obsequiously aim to please their audience with insincere words and false promises. The Prophet (ﷺ) was very different, for he was a Messenger, a Prophet who was protected from doing wrong, and one who came with wisdom, a rightly-guided set of laws, and an upright Religion. And the Prophet (ﷺ) was not like literary writers and authors, most of whom base their sayings on their personal experiences, on what they learned from other writers, on their general knowledge, and on the knowledge they gained from past thinkers. Instead, everything the Prophet (ﷺ) said about Islam came from a single source — from the Lord of all that exists.

The Goodness and Purity of the Prophet

Allah (ﷻ) said:

﴿يَـٰٓأَيُّهَا ٱلنَّبِىُّ إِنَّآ أَرْسَلْنَـٰكَ شَـٰهِدًا وَمُبَشِّرًا وَنَذِيرًا ۝ وَدَاعِيًا إِلَى ٱللَّهِ بِإِذْنِهِۦ وَسِرَاجًا مُّنِيرًا ۝﴾

(سورة الأحزاب : ٤٥-٤٦)

❨O Prophet [Muhammad]! Verily, We have sent you as a witness and a bearer of glad tidings, and a warner. And as one who invites to Allah [Islamic Monotheism, i.e. to worship none but Allah (Alone)] by His Leave, and as a lamp spreading light [through your instructions from the Qur'an and the Sunnah — the legal ways of the Prophet].❩ *(Qur'an: 33: 45,46)*

Allah (ﷻ) bestowed upon the Prophet (ﷺ) not just every single noble quality, but also every single noble quality in the highest degree possible; for instance, he was not just generous, but also generous to the highest degree possible for human beings. As such, he became an ideal role model in all areas of his life. Of all human beings, he was the humblest, the most pious, the most just, the most patient, and so on and so forth. Whereas others are good in specific areas only — patient but not generous, brave but not pious — the Prophet (ﷺ) was superlatively good in all areas, in all aspects of his noble character. And why would not that be the case, for he was sent by Allah to be an ideal role model and to guide human beings to the noblest of manners.

Sent by Allah (ﷻ) to teach others, the Prophet (ﷺ) had to himself be upon a high standard of character; and without a doubt, he certainly was upon a very high standard of character. He was good, noble, blessed, and pure. On at least a few occasions, the Prophet's heart was, as a miracle from Allah, physically removed from his body, and was then washed and purified from all evil. Consequently, his heart became innocent and free from all wicked qualities and evil feelings — such as bitterness, malice, treachery, dishonesty, and jealousy. It is not surprising, therefore, that the Prophet (ﷺ) became the most merciful, gentle, generous, and pious of all people.

﴿وَمَآ أَرْسَلْنَاكَ إِلَّا رَحْمَةً لِّلْعَلَمِينَ ۝﴾ (سورة الأنبياء: ١٠٧)

﴿And We have sent you [O Muhammad] not but as a mercy for the 'Âlameen [mankind, jinns, and all that exists'.﴾ *(Qur'an: 21: 107)*

The Prophet (ﷺ) forbade others from anger with the command, "Do not become angry", and he was the first to obey that command, staying far away from anger except when he became angry for the sake of Allah (ﷻ). Consequently, no one remembered the Prophet (ﷺ) for his anger, but everyone did remember him for his good manners, his forbearance, and his generosity — qualities they all benefited from in one way or another.

The Prophet (ﷺ) said to his Companions: "Do not be jealous of one another,"[96] and he was of course the first to apply this advice, being innocent of even the least bit of jealousy. Allah protected him from having feelings of jealousy and contempt, instilling in him instead a desire for goodness — first, guidance, and then worldly blessings — to befall all of his fellow human beings. The very people who cursed him he wanted to benefit, desiring that they should embrace Islam, so that they would, by the permission of Allah, achieve safety from the Hellfire.

The Prophet (ﷺ) said: "Do not turn your backs on one another, and do not cut off ties (of relations) from one another."[97] And he was the first to avoid the very things he forbade, by showing goodwill towards others and by performing acts of kindness to relatives and strangers alike. If someone cut off ties

---

[96] Related by Bukhari (6065, 6076) and Muslim (2559) on the authority of Anas ibn Mâlik.

[97] Refer to the footnote of the previous hadith.

from him, he tried to win over that person with acts of kindness and generosity; if someone wronged him, he forgave that person; and if someone withheld things from him, he gave generously to that person. To be sure, the following verse applies to the Prophet (ﷺ) to a greater degree than it does to any other person:

$$ ﴿ ... وَٱلْكَـٰظِمِينَ ٱلْغَيْظَ وَٱلْعَافِينَ عَنِ ٱلنَّاسِ ... ﴿١٣٤﴾ ﴾ $$

(سورة آل عِمرَان: ١٣٤)

❨... [Those] who repress anger, and who pardon men;...❩

(Qur'an: 3: 134)

In a hadith that is related in *Ṣaḥeeḥ Muslim*, the Prophet (ﷺ) said: "Verily, Allah has revealed to me (the command) that you should be humble."[98] The Prophet (ﷺ) was the epitome of humbleness. He was the Messenger of Allah (ﷺ), he had a high ranking with Allah, his Companions loved and revered him, and he was the leader of an entire Nation. In spite of all of those qualities and much else besides, the Prophet (ﷺ) would mend his own shoes, sit on the ground, milk his sheep, sit in the company of the poor, lend a helping hand to an elderly woman or a young female slave, and ride a donkey instead of a horse.

According to another hadith, he said: "The best among you is he who is the best to his family. And among you all, I am the one person who is the best to family."[99] The Prophet's wives (may Allah be pleased with them all), in the narrations they related about the Prophet (ﷺ), bore witness to this hadith. The Prophet

---

[98] Related by Muslim (2865) on the authority of 'Iyâdh ibn Humâr.

[99] Related by Tirmidhi (3895) and al-Bayhaqi, in *as-Sunan* (15477) on the authority of 'Â'ishah. And Tirmidhi said, "This hadith is *hasan, saheeh* and *Ghareeb."*

(ﷺ) was truly the best a man can be towards his wife. Whenever he visited his wives, he would bless them with his smile. He would joke around with them, and he would perform a number of household chores. He would have meaningful conversations with them, speaking to them patiently and cheerfully, without becoming harsh or rough or impatient in his tone.

﴾وَإِنَّكَ لَعَلَىٰ خُلُقٍ عَظِيمٍ ﴿٤﴾﴿

(سورة القَلَم : ٤)

﴿And verily, you [O Muhammad] are on an exalted [standard of] character.﴾ *(Qur'an: 68: 4)*

The purity of the Prophet's heart manifested itself in his judgments and in his application of justice. He didn't care who a plaintiff was and who a defendant was; had he felt that justice was on the side of someone else, he would have ruled against his relatives and friends, nay, even against his own self. He was perfectly just in his rulings; and even still, some ignorant people were not satisfied, caring not about justice, but about their own greed and ambition. On one occasion, when a man said to the Prophet (ﷺ): "Be just," the Prophet (ﷺ) became neither angry nor vindictive; instead, he replied, "I will indeed fail and lose (ultimately in the Hereafter) if I am not just. And who will be just if I am not just?"[100]

Who will be just if the Prophet (ﷺ) is not just? The answer to this question is frightening to say the least. The Prophet (ﷺ) is the most just person in the world: Therefore, had he not been just, all justice, and consequently all hope, would have been lost on earth. We can only hope that this was a point that was not lost on

---

[100] Related by Bukhari (3610) and Muslim (1063), on the authority of Abu Sa'eed al-Khudri.

the man who had so rudely said to the Prophet (ﷺ): "Be just." If justice were to take on a physical, living, breathing, speaking form, and if you were to ask it about the most just person to ever walk the earth, it most certainly would have said, "Muhammad (ﷺ)."

When a person's heart is not pure, he may rule justly between two strangers, but he will not rule justly when his own interests — or the interests of his loved ones — are at stake. But the Prophet's heart was pure; furthermore, it was free from every manifestation of evil. Therefore, he was just even at the expense of his own benefit and comfort, and even at the expense of the people he loved the most. He once swore that, were his daughter Fâṭimah (﵂) to steal, he would have taken it upon himself to cut off her hand. And on certain occasions, when he felt that he had wronged someone — even though he never did wrong anyone — he would ask the person he felt he had wronged to exact revenge against him.

These days, one can get away with the worst of crimes as long as one is properly connected — to someone who is close to the leader of a country, to a prince, to a senator, to a very rich man, etc. If a prince's nephew perpetrates a crime, he receives no punishment; but if an ordinary person perpetrates the same crime, he spends years in prison. The opposite held true during the Prophet's lifetime. A female member of the Quraysh — who was from the Banu Makhzoom clan — committed the crime of stealing. And when it was decided that her hand should be cut off, the people of the Quraysh turned to a man whom the Prophet (ﷺ) loved dearly and asked him to intercede on behalf of the female thief. That man was Usâmah ibn Zayd (﵁). Reluctantly, Usâmah agreed to intercede on behalf of the Makhzoomi woman. When he finally brought up the matter to the Prophet (ﷺ), the color of the Prophet's face turned crimson. In an angry tone, the Messenger of Allah (ﷺ) said: "Are you interceding regarding one of Allah's decreed laws (or punishments)?" Immediately realizing the mistake he had made, Usâmah said, "Ask forgiveness for me, O Messenger of Allah!"[101]

On another occasion, Zubayr (ﷺ) and a man from the Anṣâr appeared as litigants before the Prophet (ﷺ). When the Prophet (ﷺ) ruled in favor of Zubayr, the Anṣâri man complained, saying that the Prophet (ﷺ) ruled against him because Zubayr was the son of the Prophet's aunt, Ṣafiyyah. Allah (ﷻ) then revealed the following verse:

$$\text{﴿فَلَا وَرَبِّكَ لَا يُؤْمِنُونَ حَتَّىٰ يُحَكِّمُوكَ فِيمَا شَجَرَ بَيْنَهُمْ ثُمَّ لَا يَجِدُوا فِي أَنفُسِهِمْ حَرَجًا مِّمَّا قَضَيْتَ وَيُسَلِّمُوا تَسْلِيمًا ﴾}$$

(سورة النِّساء: ٦٥)

﴿But no, by your Lord, they can have no Faith, until they make you [O Muhammad] judge in all disputes between them, and find in themselves no resistance against your decisions, and accept [them] with full submission.﴾ *(Qur'an 4: 65)*

Sufficient was Allah (ﷻ), therefore, as a witness to the justice and fairness of the Messenger of Allah (ﷺ).

The Prophet (ﷺ) came to establish justice and to eradicate injustice on earth, a point that is agreed upon by the Prophet's enemies and friends alike. The very people who disbelieved in him in Makkah entrusted him with their valuables, not deeming

---

[101] Related by Bukhari (3475, 6788), on the authority of 'Â'ishah.

any other person trustworthy enough for the job. And the very same Jews who rejected his message would come to him and ask him to judge between them in their disputes.

The Prophet's purity also manifested itself in his good manners and handsome appearance. As for his manners, his deeds bore witness to what he said; his inner self corroborated his outward deeds; and his limbs bore witness to what was in his heart. And as for his appearance, he was the handsomest of people. His face was illuminated, his skin was soft, his breath was like Musk (the best kind of perfume), the odor that emanated from his body was good and pure, and even his sweat was beautiful, trickling down his skin like pearls. Anas (صلى الله عليه وسلم) said: "I have never touched any silk or *Deebâj* (a kind of silk) that was softer than the hand of the Prophet (صلى الله عليه وسلم), and I have never smelled any fragrance or scent that was better than the fragrance or scent of the Prophet (صلى الله عليه وسلم)."[102] After shaking the Prophet's hand, a man would, for a number of days that followed, continue to smell on himself the sweet smell of the Prophet's fragrance.

A person whose heart is not pure does not smile, but instead frowns. Such a person is certainly not good company, for he is often grumpy and in foul humor. As for the Prophet (صلى الله عليه وسلم), his heart was pure; consequently, he was very good company: Upon hearing something funny, he would laugh; upon meeting someone, he would have a smile on his face; upon seeing something sad, he would cry and console a person who was grief-stricken. And when he would sit in a gathering, he would fill the hearts of all who were present with happiness and a feeling of peace. No one ever felt bored by his speech, and no one ever grew

---

[102] Related by Bukhari (3561) and Muslim (2330), on the authority of Anas.

weary of his company; on the contrary, anyone who knew him found it virtually unbearable to part company from him.

On the Muslim holiday of 'Eid, the Prophet (ﷺ) would go out, wearing both a beautiful garment and a pleasant smile. For his Companions, 'Eid was, without a doubt, an enjoyable holiday; but any day they saw the Prophet (ﷺ), sat in his company, or listened to his blessed words was a holiday in itself, an occasion of joy and happiness. In fact, just to look at the Prophet (ﷺ) reminded them of Allah (ﷻ).

The purity of the Prophet's heart also manifested itself on the battlefield. A person with an impure heart is afraid of dying, his heart being full of doubts and evil thoughts. As for the Prophet (ﷺ), he longed to meet his Lord; and so for him, the Hereafter was much better than this life. Consequently, he fought with both skill and bravery, fighting in the front lines and never retreating from the enemy. Even the bravest of Companions, those who were known for their prowess on the battlefield, would stand behind the Prophet (ﷺ) when the fighting in a battle intensified, when it seemed most likely that the enemy would gain the upper hand. They somehow knew that, as long as they remained near the Prophet (ﷺ), they would be safe and victory would be theirs.

Muhammad, the beloved Prophet

﴿ ... فَٱلَّذِينَ ءَامَنُوا بِهِۦ وَعَزَّرُوهُ وَنَصَرُوهُ وَٱتَّبَعُوا ٱلنُّورَ ٱلَّذِىٓ أُنزِلَ مَعَهُۥٓ ... ﴿١٥٧﴾ ﴾

(سورة الأعراف : ١٥٧)

◄... So those who believe in him [Muhammad], honor him, help him, and follow the light [the Qur'an] which has been sent down with him...► *(Qur'an: 7: 157)*

In a hadith that is related in *Ṣaḥeeḥ Bukhari*, the Messenger of Allah (ﷺ) said: "One of you does not believe until I become more beloved to him than his children, his father, and all people."[103]

Whoever studies the biographies of the Companions knows of the profound love they felt for the Prophet (ﷺ), a love that controlled their every emotion; a love that cannot be matched by the love that a person feels towards his son, his father, his mother, or his wife; a love that reached the innermost regions of their hearts.

But why did they love him so much? This is a legitimate question, for throughout history no group of people have loved their leader, their king, their spiritual guide, or anyone else for that matter as much as the Companions loved Prophet Muhammad (ﷺ). They tried their best to imitate his every action, and they obeyed his every command. They were willing to use their bodies as human shields to protect him, and they were willing to do anything to protect not just his life, but his honor as well. Some of them were in such awe of the Prophet (ﷺ) that they were never able to look directly at his face — to fix their gaze on him long enough to get a clear image of him. In answer to his command some of them went out to foreign lands, knowing that certain death awaited them at the hands of Islam's enemies; and yet they were happy to leave, as if they were going to spend their first night with a new bride — such was the degree to which they loved the

---

[103] Related by Bukhari (15) and Muslim (44), on the authority of Anas.

Prophet (ﷺ) and believed in his message. In every possible way, they preferred the Prophet (ﷺ) over their own selves: they preferred his happiness over their own happiness; they desired his comfort, even if it meant that they had to struggle and work hard; and they desired that he should eat his fill, even if that meant they would have to go hungry. They would not raise their voices over the voice of the Prophet (ﷺ), and they would never force their opinion upon him or decide to do something without first seeking his decision and then submitting to it. They loved him, they obeyed him, they were in awe of him, and they strove to follow every aspect of his Sunnah. As for the causes of their love for him, well, there are many causes — the greatest of them being that he was not just a man, but he was also the Messenger of the Most Merciful; he was the chosen one from mankind and jinns. Allah sent him to take mankind out of the darkness of disbelief, and to bring them into the light of true Islamic Monotheism. And Allah (ﷻ) sent him to take people by the hand and to lead them to Paradise, which is as wide as the heavens and the earth.

And they loved him not just because he was a Messenger of Allah (ﷻ) — even though that was the main reason why they loved him — but also because of his noble qualities and wonderful manners. He won them over with the wonderful way in which he dealt with them and with the kindness and generosity that he constantly bestowed upon them. In spending time with him, they constantly felt spiritual elation and a strengthening of their Faith. They felt this way after having spent years wandering in darkness, disbelief, and ignorance. He, after all, was the one who washed their souls — by the permission of Allah — from the filth of polytheism. He was the one who purified their insides from the sins of disbelief, and who washed their hearts from the shame of worshipping idols. He (ﷺ) taught them how to lead a noble life, and he filled their breasts with happiness after they had spent years feeling confused and miserable. He built in their hearts fortresses of Faith, after their hearts had been a barren wasteland of doubt and misguidance.

Before he came to them with his message, they lived like wandering beasts: they had no faith, no manners, no prayer, no charity, no light, and no righteousness. Theirs was a gloomy and dark life which involved worshipping false idols, perpetrating lewd acts, senselessly imbibing large quantities of alcohol, needlessly spilling the blood of innocent people, and constantly plundering and destroying one another's villages and towns. They had no purpose, no real reason to wake up every morning, for they did not know Allah — and there is no true life without knowledge of Allah (ﷻ). And they knew nothing of the Hereafter; they simply wandered in their misguidance, wasting away the hours and days of their empty lives, and waiting for their insignificant deaths.

They had hearts that were harder than stones, and souls that were darker than the darkest part of the night. They did not contemplate the universe around them; they did not care about the sanctity of human life; they did not care whether they gained wealth through honest or dishonest means; they, as a people, did not uphold any higher principles or values.

When Allah willed to save them, to bring them happiness, and to bestow upon them success, He (ﷻ) sent Muhammad (ﷺ) to them. Then, it was as if they were reborn, and it was as if the world was born anew as well. Revelation began to descend upon the Prophet (ﷺ), and Jibreel (ﷺ) would go back and forth, between the heavens and the earth, always bringing new teachings

of the divine law that was being revealed to Prophet Muhammad
(ﷺ). That divine law meant happiness for Allah's slaves and
uprightness for the community of Muslims. Thereafter, good
deeds, after a long period of being absent on earth, began to be
performed on a regular basis: Masjids began to be built, slaves
began to be freed, hearts began to be filled with knowledge and
Faith, bodies began to be purified, and prayer began to be
performed. The Qur'an was now recited and studied, and sayings
of the Prophet (ﷺ) were now being collected and disseminated
among students of knowledge. Furthermore, an entire nation
became freed from the shackles of slavery to other created beings,
and the most beautiful civilization the world has ever known
began to develop and flourish.

﴿هُوَ ٱلَّذِى بَعَثَ فِى ٱلۡأُمِّيِّـۧنَ رَسُولًا مِّنۡهُمۡ يَتۡلُواْ عَلَيۡهِمۡ ءَايَٰتِهِۦ وَيُزَكِّيهِمۡ وَيُعَلِّمُهُمُ
ٱلۡكِتَٰبَ وَٱلۡحِكۡمَةَ وَإِن كَانُواْ مِن قَبۡلُ لَفِى ضَلَٰلٍ مُّبِينٍ ٢﴾   (سورة الجُمُعَة : ٢)

﴿He it is Who sent among the unlettered ones a Messenger
[Muhammad] from among themselves, reciting to them His Verses,
purifying them [from the filth of disbelief and polytheism], and
teaching them the Book [this Qur'an, Islamic Laws and Islamic
Jurisprudence] and al-Ḥikmah [Sunnah: legal ways, orders, acts of
worship of Prophet Muhammad]. And verily, they have been before
in manifest error.﴾   (Qur'an: 62: 2)

The Companions loved the Messenger of Allah (ﷺ)
because it was through him that they came to know Allah (ﷻ),
and because it was he who informed them about what they had to
do in order to gain the Good Pleasure of Allah. Loving the Prophet
(ﷺ) was the least the Companions could do to honor him, for he
was the one who showed them the straight path that leads to
Paradise and warned them against every form of misguidance, and

against anything that leads to the Hellfire. He was the one who said to them, "O people, say, 'None has the right to be worshipped but Allah,' and you will succeed."[104] Regarding Prayer, he said to them: "Pray as you have seen me pray."[105] Regarding Ḥajj, he said to them: "Take from me your rites (of Ḥajj)."[106] He taught them his Sunnah, and he said to them: "Whosoever turns away from my Sunnah (my way, my guidance, etc.) is not from me."[107] And he exhorted them to fear Allah, saying to them: "The person among you who fears Allah the most and is most knowledgeable about Allah, is me."[108] Through the Prophet (ﷺ), Allah saved the Companions from the Hellfire; through him, Allah saved them from spiritual blindness and misguidance; and through him, Allah (ﷻ) saved them from ignorance.

How could the Companions, nay, how could Muslims in general, not love the Prophet (ﷺ) when he is the ideal role model for all of their good deeds? When one performs any act of worship — be it ablution, prayer, fasting, charity, Ḥajj, remembering Allah — one has to first imagine how the Prophet (ﷺ) performed that act of worship, and only then can one perform that act of worship properly. How can Muslims not love the Prophet (ﷺ) when he is a guide, teacher, and example for them in every aspect of their lives?

How can Muslims not love the Prophet (ﷺ) when he invited people, through his sayings and actions, to everything that

---

[104] Related by Aḥmad (18525) and al-Ḥâkim (39), on the authority of Rabee‘ah ibn ‘Abbâd.

[105] Related by Bukhari (631), on the authority of Mâlik ibn al-Huwayrith.

[106] Related by Muslim (1297), on the authority of Jâbir ibn ‘Abdullâh.

[107] Related by Bukhari (5063) and Muslim (1401), on the authority of Anas.

[108] Related by Bukhari (20), on the authority of ‘Â’ishah.

is good and virtuous — truthfulness, justice, peace, mercy, brotherhood, generosity, etc.? And how can Muslims not love the Prophet (ﷺ) when he warned them, and tried to save them, from all forms of evil — such as oppression, transgression, and injustice. The day one starts practicing the teachings of Islam, the day upon which one begins to follow the example of the Messenger of Allah (ﷺ) is the day one is truly born.

The happiness of every individual on earth hinges upon following the example of the Prophet (ﷺ), since he alone, of all human beings, was upon the truth in everything he said and did. All of our sayings and deeds must first be scrutinized in order to see whether they are in accordance with his sayings and deeds, for he is the standard of all that is good, and his Sunnah is the yardstick by which all else is measured.

❨And verily, you [O Muhammad] are indeed guiding [mankind] to the Straight Path [i.e., Allah's Religion of Islamic Monotheism].❩
(Qur'an 42: 52)

Muhammad, the blessed one

﴿وَجَعَلَنِي مُبَارَكًا أَيْنَ مَا كُنتُ وَأَوْصَنِي بِٱلصَّلَوٰةِ وَٱلزَّكَوٰةِ مَا دُمْتُ حَيًّا ۝﴾ (سورة مَريَم: ٣١)

❨And He has made me blessed wheresoever I be, and has enjoined on me *Salât* [prayer], and Zakah, as long as I live.❩ *(Qur'an: 19: 31)*

The Prophet (ﷺ) was blessed in every possible way: he was blessed in himself, he had blessings with him, and blessings accompanied him wherever he went throughout his life. His speech was blessed. He had the uncanny ability of saying a single phrase that conveyed profound meanings and beautiful lessons. What he conveyed in a single minute another man could only convey in hours, if not days — such was the eloquence of the Prophet (ﷺ).

He was blessed in his life span as well. He was a Prophet for only twenty-three years, and yet what did he accomplish during that short span of time? In that short period, he spread Islam, knowledge, and guidance throughout the world. In short, he accomplished what all other men could not accomplish in decades, or even in centuries. In twenty-three short years, the Prophet (ﷺ) conveyed the message of Islam, taught the Qur'an, established a set of precedents which became known as his Sunnah, eradicated disbelief in the Arabian peninsula, established a stable country that he founded upon the principle of justice, and built the most wonderful and the most rightly-guided civilization that mankind has ever known.

Consider the blessedness of a single day of his life. Let us go back to the Day of *an-Nahr*, the thirteenth day of his Ḥajj (i.e., his pilgrimage to Makkah). On that day, the Prophet (ﷺ) prayed *Fajr* at Muzdalifah; then he set out for Mina, all the while remembering Allah, glorifying Him, supplicating to Him, teaching people the rights of Ḥajj, and providing legal rulings for pilgrims who came to him with questions. Then the Prophet (ﷺ) threw pebbles at Jamaratul-'Aqabah. Next, he shaved his head, and then he slaughtered his sacrificial animal. Then he went to the Inviolable Masjid and performed *Ṭawâf* (i.e., walking around the Ka'bah a number of times as an act of worship). Then the Prophet (ﷺ) prayed <u>*Dhuhr*</u>. This is what the Prophet (ﷺ) accomplished not in an entire day, but just from *Fajr* prayer until <u>*Dhuhr*</u> prayer — an amazing feat, to be sure, especially considering the facts that his means of transportation was not a car, but instead his riding camel; that the places he went to were separated from each other considerable distances; that the places he visited were extremely crowded, since many thousands of people accompanied the Prophet (ﷺ) during his pilgrimage; that it was a very hot day; and that people continually interrupted the Prophet's progress, in order to ask him legal questions about the pilgrimage in particular, and perhaps about Islam in general. So Glory be to Allah, Who made the short years of the Prophet's life so blessed, and so filled with productivity and accomplishments.

By the Permission and the Grace of Allah (ﷻ), the Prophet (ﷺ) was blessed in the effect he had on people and things. For instance, he one once passed by the graves of two men who were being punished. One of them was being punished because he did not clean himself properly after he urinated; and the other was being punished because he was a talebearer, a man who would go from person to person spreading slander. Standing over their graves, the Prophet (ﷺ) broke a green branch into two and planted the two pieces into the ground, above the two men's graves. The Prophet (ﷺ) then said: "I hope that this will decrease their punishment at least until these two (sticks) become dry."[109] This was something specific to the Prophet (ﷺ): only he, because he was blessed by Allah (ﷻ), was able to have such a blessed effect in his actions.

---

[109] Related by Bukhari (216, 218) and Muslim (292), on the authority of Ibn 'Abbâs.

On the day of Khaybar, 'Ali ibn Abi Ṭâlib (ﷺ) felt pain in his eyes, to the point that he literally lost his vision, not being able to see anything at all. The Prophet (ﷺ) then spit into his eyes. No sooner did the Prophet (ﷺ) do that than 'Ali's vision returned completely to normal by the permission of Allah.

And during the siege of al-Khandaq, the Prophet (ﷺ) had with him an army that consisted of one thousand men. As the siege intensified, the supplies of the Muslims in Madeenah became depleted to the point that Muslim soldiers began to lack basic nourishment. During that difficult period of time, Jâbir ibn 'Abdullâh (ﷺ) invited the Prophet (ﷺ) and three others to a simple meal that his wife had prepared for them. The meal was barely enough for four or five people, and yet the Prophet (ﷺ) invited all of the members of his army to partake in the meal. Initially, Jâbir was surprised to say the least, because he could not understand how such little food would be enough for so many people. The Prophet (ﷺ) blew into the food and then began to invite soldiers inside, ten at a time. The food became blessed, increasing in quantity, to the point that every single member of the Muslim army ate until he became full; and even after that, there was much food leftover, food that was then distributed among the various households of Madeenah. On that evening, every single household in Madeenah had a share of the blessed food. None has the right to be worshipped but Allah! Oh what a wonderful miracle and a clear proof that was of the truthfulness of the Prophet (ﷺ), of his blessedness, and of his Prophethood.

On another occasion, the Prophet (ﷺ) went abroad on a military expedition, taking with him an army that consisted of 1400 men. During the course of their journey, while being in the middle of the desert, they ran out of water, and were on the verge of complete annihilation. When the situation looked bleakest, the Prophet (ﷺ) asked for a container that contained a small quantity of water. He then poured that water onto his pure, blessed hands, and to the amazement of everyone, streams of water began to gush forth from between his fingers. The members of the army not only filled all of their containers with that blessed water, but also used the water to provide drink to their riding animals. Everyone drank, performed ablution, and even used the water to take baths.

﴿أَفَسِحْرٌ هَٰذَآ أَمْ أَنتُمْ لَا تُبْصِرُونَ ۝﴾ (سورة الطُّور: ١٥)

﴿Is this magic or do you not see?﴾ *(Qur'an: 52: 15)*

One day, Sa'd ibn Abi Waqqâṣ (ﻋ) became very ill. His temperature rose to such a high level that he felt that his body was burning up. The Prophet (ﷺ) visited him and placed his blessed hand on Sa'd's chest. In an instant, Sa'd went from feeling a burning sensation to feeling a cooling sensation, as if ice had been placed on his chest. And he became cured by the permission of Allah (ﷻ). Years later, Sa'd recalled that day, saying, "By Allah, until this very moment it is as if I can feel the coolness of his hand on my chest."

On another occasion, when Jâbir ibn 'Abdullâh (ﻋ) fell ill, the Prophet (ﷺ) performed ablution and sprinkled the water that was left over onto Jâbir, who, by the permission of Allah (ﷻ), immediately became cured of his illness. And when he (ﷺ) was at Mina on the day of *an-Naḥr*, the Prophet (ﷺ) shaved his head and gave all of the hair on the right side of his head to Abu Ṭalḥah al-Anṣâri (ﻋ). Because Abu Ṭalḥah possessed a powerful voice, and because he used that voice to call out to soldiers during battles, giving them important instructions and encouraging them to fight bravely, the Prophet (ﷺ) rewarded him by giving him all of the hair on the right side of his head. The Prophet (ﷺ) gave him that hair because every part of him was blessed; he wanted to give Abu Ṭalḥah the opportunity to use his hair as a means of blessing himself in whatever way he wanted. As for the hair on the left half of the Prophet's head, the Prophet (ﷺ) distributed it among all of the other pilgrims who were with him. And as that hair was being distributed, people literally were fighting with one another over it. Some of them got a few hairs; others got a single hair; and yet others had to share a single strand of hair among two or more people. In order to be blessed by the Prophet (ﷺ), some of them would place his hairs in water and then drink that water. Such was the blessedness of the Prophet (ﷺ).

When Abu Maḥdhoorah (ﷺ) was a young child, the Prophet (ﷺ) gently and mercifully passed his hand over his head. Abu Maḥdhoorah then made an oath never to shave or cut the hair that had been touched by the blessed hand of the Messenger of Allah (ﷺ). Abu Maḥdhoorah then let his hair grow for the duration of his life, until it became very long indeed; and when he died, he was buried with that hair.

And children would go to the Prophet (ﷺ) with their containers of milk and water, asking him to place his blessed hand inside, knowing that that would bring blessings and cures for their illnesses, by the permission of Allah (ﷺ). The stories of the Prophet's blessedness are countless, and there is no end to the number of *Aḥâdeeth* that contain accounts of the Prophet's miracles. To be sure, he was blessed wherever he was, and wherever he went. O Allah, send prayers and salutations on Prophet Muhammad, on his family, and on his Companions.

How the Prophet spiritually nurtured his Companions

*A*llah (ﷺ) said:

﴿ ... يَتْلُواْ عَلَيْهِمْ ءَايَٰتِهِۦ وَيُزَكِّيهِمْ وَيُعَلِّمُهُمُ ٱلْكِتَٰبَ وَٱلْحِكْمَةَ ... ﴾

(سورة آل عِمرَان: ١٦٤)

﴿... Reciting unto them His Verses [the Qur'an], and purifying them [from sins by their following him], and instructing them [in] the Book [the Qur'an] and *al-Ḥikmah* [the wisdom and the Sunnah of the Prophet, i.e., his legal ways, statements, acts of worship, etc.]...﴾

(Qur'an 3: 164)

Every good teacher knows how to reach out to his students, how to bring out from them their full potential. In this regard — as in all other regards — none was, or ever will be, better than the Messenger of Allah (ﷺ). In teaching others, he was gentle, and he exhorted others to be gentle as well: "Verily, Allah is *Rafeeq* (Kind, Merciful, Gentle), and He loves gentleness. And Allah gives for gentleness that which He does not give for harshness."[110] According to another narration, the Prophet (ﷺ) said: "Whenever gentleness is present in something, it beautifies it; when gentleness is removed from something, that thing becomes spoiled."[111]

---

[110] Related by Bukhari (6927) and Muslim (2593), on the authority of 'Â'ishah.

[111] Related by Muslim (2594), on the authority of 'Â'ishah.

Because of the Prophet's noble manners, others were drawn to him, wishing that they could remain in his company all the time. Allah (ﷻ) said:

﴿فَبِمَا رَحْمَةٍ مِّنَ ٱللَّهِ لِنتَ لَهُمْ وَلَوْ كُنتَ فَظًّا غَلِيظَ ٱلْقَلْبِ لَٱنفَضُّوا۟ مِنْ حَوْلِكَ فَٱعْفُ عَنْهُمْ وَٱسْتَغْفِرْ لَهُمْ وَشَاوِرْهُمْ فِى ٱلْأَمْرِ فَإِذَا عَزَمْتَ فَتَوَكَّلْ عَلَى ٱللَّهِ إِنَّ ٱللَّهَ يُحِبُّ ٱلْمُتَوَكِّلِينَ ۝﴾ (سورة آل عِمرَان: ١٥٩)

﴿And by the Mercy of Allah, you dealt with them gently. And had you been severe and harsh-hearted, they would have broken away from about you; so pass over [their faults], and ask [Allah's] Forgiveness for them; and consult them in the affairs. Then when you have taken a decision, put your trust in Allah, certainly, Allah loves those who put their trust [in Him].﴾   *(Qur'an 3: 159)*

One day, a Bedouin entered the Masjid and said during the *Tashâhud* (the part of the Prayer during which one is seated on the ground), "O Allah, have mercy on me and on Muhammad, and do not have mercy on anyone other than us." The Prophet (ﷺ) then pointed out that it was wrong of him to limit Allah's mercy to just two people, since Allah's mercy is vast and encompasses all things. The Prophet (ﷺ) said, "Verily, you have made narrow that which is wide and vast."[112]

The Bedouin then stood up, moved towards a corner of the Masjid, and then proceeded to urinate — casually and unselfconsciously, as if what he was doing was perfectly normal. The Companions of the Messenger of Allah said: "*Mah Mah* (An expression used to severely scold someone, to indicate the graveness of a matter)." The Messenger of Allah (ﷺ) said, "Do

---

[112] Related by Bukhari (6010), on the authority of Abu Hurayrah.

not put a halt to his urinating, but instead leave him." They left him alone until he finished urinating. Then the Messenger of Allah (ﷺ) called him and said to him, "Any kind of urine or filth is not suitable for these Masâjid; instead, they (i.e., Masâjid) are only (appropriate) for the remembrance of Allah, the Prayer, and the recitation of the Qur'an."[113] Greatly moved by the gentleness and kindness of the Prophet (ﷺ), the Bedouin returned to his people and invited them to Islam. And by the Grace and Mercy of Allah (ﷺ), they accepted his invitation by entering into the fold of Islam.

The Prophet (ﷺ) was not gentle with the rich and the strong only to be harsh with the poor and the weak; on the contrary, the Prophet (ﷺ) was gentle with everyone — even with children. One day during meal-time, a young boy reached out with his hand, taking food from all parts of a dish. In Islam, it is proper etiquette for a person to eat from that part of a plate or dish that is nearest to him. But even though the young boy breached the Islamic etiquette of eating, the Prophet (ﷺ) neither scolded him nor sent him away; instead, with kindness and gentleness, he corrected the boy's mistake, saying to him: "O young boy, say Allah's Name (before you eat), eat with your right hand, and eat from what is nearest to you."[114]

'Â'ishah (ﷺ) related that a group of Jews once went to the Prophet (ﷺ) and said: "As-Sâm (Death) be upon you, O Abul-Qâsim." As-Sâm sounds similar to as-Salâm, but the former means death and the latter means peace. They were hoping that the Prophet (ﷺ) would not discern their secret curse, but he did,

---

[113] Related by Muslim (285), on the authority of Anas ibn Mâlik.
[114] Related by Bukhari (5376, 5378) and Muslim (2022), on the authority of 'Umar ibn Abi Salamah.

and so did 'Â'ishah, who, becoming angry, said, "And as-Sâm (Death) be upon you, and may Allah do with you (such and such in order to punish you)." The Messenger of Allah (ﷺ) said, "Be quiet, O' 'Â'ishah, for indeed, Allah does not love al-Faḥsh and at-Tafâhush (i.e., foul speech and deeds, and the foul speech and deeds that are done in an intentional and affected manner)." 'Â'ishah said, "O Messenger of Allah, you do see what they are saying?" The Prophet (ﷺ) said, "Do you not see that I return back to them that which they say, if I say, 'And (the same) upon you.' "[115] What this means is that, regardless of whether they had said as-Sâm or as-Salâm, the Prophet (ﷺ) would be giving them an appropriate answer by saying, "And the same upon you," without having to resort to bad manners and the use of foul language.

The Prophet (ﷺ) did not overload his Companions with information; he did not force them to listen to lectures a few times a day or even once a day — although such a schedule of lectures would certainly have pleased them. The Prophet (ﷺ) was afraid that his Companions would become bored with daily, lengthy lectures, and so he would leave a sufficient gap between one lecture or sermon and the next; such a gap allowed the Companions to regain a sense of enthusiasm, so that they would yearn for another sermon, one that would give them the spiritual fuel they needed until the sermon that came after it. And even when the Prophet (ﷺ) did deliver a sermon, he would be economical with his words, giving a sermon that was at once meaningful and brief. And he exhorted others to follow the same standard; he said: "Verily, the prolongation of a man's prayer and

---

[115] Related by Bukhari (2935, 6030) and Muslim (2165), on the authority of 'Â'ishah.

the brevity of his sermon are signs of his understanding (Fiqh)."[116]

When 'Umar (رضي الله عنه) reproached a group of Abyssinians for playing with spears in the Masjid, the Prophet (ﷺ) said: "O 'Umar, leave them, so that the Jews can know that there is spaciousness (a large degree of leeway to enjoy the lawful things of life) in our Religion."[117]

One year, on the Muslim holiday of 'Eid, Abu Bakr (رضي الله عنه) visited the Prophet (ﷺ), who, at the time, was in 'Â'ishah's apartment. When Abu Bakr entered, two girls were inside, and they were both singing. Abu Bakr exclaimed: "The singing (or the flute noises) of *Shaytân* in the presence of the Prophet!" The Messenger of Allah (ﷺ) then said, "Leave them be, O Abu Bakr; for indeed, every group of people has a holiday, and this is our holiday."[118]

The Prophet (ﷺ) once asked 'Â'ishah (رضي الله عنها) about a marriage banquet she had attended; that particular marriage took place between members of the Anṣâr. The Prophet (ﷺ) asked: "Was there among you some form of entertainment, for indeed, the people of the Anṣâr like entertainment."[119] The entertainment the Prophet (ﷺ) referred to was, of course, lawful entertainment — the kind of innocent diversion that rejuvenates the soul and provides a healthy break from serious affairs and hard work. As

---

[116] Related by Muslim (869), on the authority of 'Ammâr.

[117] Related by Aḥmad (24334, 25431), on the authority of 'Â'ishah; refer also to *Kashf al-Khifâ* (658).

[118] Related by Bukhari (952, 3931) and Muslim (892), on the authority of 'Â'ishah.

[119] Related by Bukhari (5163), on the authority of 'Â'ishah.

for what is forbidden in Islam, no one stayed further away from the unlawful than the Prophet (ﷺ).

The Prophet (ﷺ) used many effective methods of teaching — such as repeating what he said three times, giving commands that were at once brief and easy-to-memorize, and changing the pitch of his tone depending on the importance of what he was saying. But the best method of teaching that the Prophet (ﷺ) employed — and that every good teacher employs — is that of being a good role model. The Prophet (ﷺ) taught his Companions to fear Allah, and he taught them not just with words, but also with his character, for he feared Allah more than anyone from among them. When he would forbid his Companions from a certain action, he would be more careful to avoid that action than any other person. When he reminded them to fear Allah and to think about the Hereafter, tears could be seen flowing down his noble cheeks. He advised them to adopt noble manners, and he himself had the best of manners. He encouraged them to remember Allah frequently, and no one remembered Allah more than he did. He exhorted them to give generously, and no one was more generous than he was. He advised them to be good to their families, and no one was better to his family than the Prophet (ﷺ) was to his family. In short, every religious teaching that the Prophet (ﷺ) commanded others to follow, he followed himself.

Consequently, what the Prophet (ﷺ) taught his Companions (may Allah be pleased with them) had a long-lasting effect on them. They continued to remember everything he said for as long as they lived, not only applying his teachings, but also passing them on to the next generation of Muslims. As a teacher, the Prophet (ﷺ) had such a profound impact on others that if a person met him, believed in him, and spent even a single hour with him, the effect of that meeting would remain with that person for the rest of his life; in fact, for that person, it was as if the only day that was truly worth remembering was the day he had spent with the Prophet (ﷺ). And that is because of the Prophet's truthfulness, sincerity, blessedness, and noble manners.

Sending Prayers upon the Prophet

﴿إِنَّ ٱللَّهَ وَمَلَٰٓئِكَتَهُۥ يُصَلُّونَ عَلَى ٱلنَّبِيِّ يَٰٓأَيُّهَا ٱلَّذِينَ ءَامَنُوا۟ صَلُّوا۟ عَلَيْهِ وَسَلِّمُوا۟ تَسْلِيمًا ٥٦﴾

(سورة الأحزاب : ٥٦)

﴿Allah sends His *Ṣalât* [Graces, Honours, Blessings, Mercy] on the Prophet [Muḥammad], and also His angels [ask Allah to bless and forgive him]. O you who believe! Send your *Ṣalât* on [ask Allah to bless] him [Muḥammad], and [you should] greet [salute] him with the Islamic way of greeting [salutations i.e. *as-Salâmu 'Alaykum*].﴾

(Qur'an: 33: 56)

Sending prayers upon the Prophet (ﷺ) has a profoundly positive effect on a person's life. When one sends prayers upon the Prophet (ﷺ), one feels a sense of calmness, of tranquillity, and of peace. When one sends prayers upon the Prophet (ﷺ), one's worries and troubles disappear. When a person sends prayers upon the Prophet (ﷺ), happiness and joy pervade that person's soul. And when one sends prayers upon the Prophet (ﷺ) in a gathering, that gathering becomes blessed, and peace and tranquillity descend upon it. Sending prayers upon the Prophet (ﷺ) is a sign of one's love, a testament to one's faith and loyalty to the Prophet (ﷺ), and a clear indication of one's love for Allah, the Exalted, the Almighty — for to love Allah truly, one must love and follow the Prophet (ﷺ).

The Prophet (ﷺ) said: "Whosoever sends a prayer upon me (i.e., whoever invokes Allah to mention me in a good way in the highest company of angels), then Allah will send *Ṣalât* upon him (i.e., will show mercy to him, will increase his rewards, or will mention him in a good way in the highest company of angels) ten times. And Allah will raise him by ten rankings. Also, ten good deeds will be recorded for him, and ten evil deeds will be erased from him (from his record)."[120] In another hadith, the Prophet (ﷺ) said: "Send many prayers upon me on the night before Friday and on the day of Friday."[121] In yet another hadith, the Prophet (ﷺ) said: "Shame on the person (the literal wording is 'May his nose be rubbed in dirt') in whose presence I am mentioned, but who does not then send prayers upon me."[122]

It is further related that the Prophet (ﷺ) said: "The miserly person is he in whose company I am mentioned, but does not send prayers upon me."[123] It is related that the Prophet (ﷺ) also said, "Verily, Allah has angels that travel throughout the earth and convey to me greetings of peace from the people of my

---

[120] Related by Nasâ'i, in *al-Kubrâ* (9890), and in *'Amal al-Yawm wal-Laylah* (63), on the authority of Anas ibn Mâlik.

[121] Related by Ibn 'Adi, in *al-Kâmil* (3/102); by al-Bayhaqi, in *al-Kubrâ* (5790) and *ash-Shu'ab al-Eemâm* (3030), on the authority of Anas ibn Mâlik; refer also to *Kashf al-Khifâ* (1/190).

[122] Related by Aḥmad (7402), Tirmidhi (3545), and al-Ḥâkim (2016), on the authority of Abu Hurayrah.

[123] Related by Aḥmad (1738) and Tirmidhi (3546), on the authority of 'Ali; refer also to *Kashf al-Khifâ* (1/332).

Nation."[124] And when Ubay ibn Ka'b (⌦) said, "I will make my entire Prayer (i.e., supplication) for you," the Prophet (⌦) replied, "Then your sin(s) will be forgiven, and your worries will be taken care of."[125]

Sending prayers upon the Prophet (⌦) is not a deed that any of us should take lightly; in fact, as Muslims, sending prayers upon the Prophet (⌦) is one of the best deeds that we can perform, and it is also one of the deeds we should perform very frequently. We should send prayers upon the Prophet (⌦) when we remember him; during the Friday Sermon; during 'Eid, the holiday of Muslims; when we pray for rain; when one of us reads the sermon of marriage; in gatherings of knowledge; in books, letters, contracts, and any other kind of agreement or treaty; when we meet our loved ones; when we part from our fellow Muslims in order to embark on a journey; when we supplicate to Allah, asking Him for help and guidance; when we say morning and evening invocations; when we are afflicted with sadness or a calamity; when we hear good news; when we speak about his biography, and on a number of other occasions besides. O Allah, send prayers upon the Prophet along as day follows night, and night follows day; as long as rain continues to fall from the sky; as long as fruits and trees grow on earth; and as long as stars are seen in the sky. O Allah, send prayers on Prophet Muhammad, on his pure and noble family, on his pious Companions from the *Muhâjiroon* and the Anṣâr, and on those who follow them upon righteousness and goodness.

---

[124] Related by Aḥmad (3657, 4198), Nasâ'i (1282), ad-Dârimi (2774), and al-Ḥâkim (3576), on the authority of 'Abdullâh ibn Mas'ood.

[125] Related by Tirmidhi (2457), who said, "This hadith is *hasan ṣaheeh*."

The importance of showing good manners to the Prophet

﴿يَـٰٓأَيُّهَا ٱلَّذِينَ ءَامَنُوا۟ لَا تَرْفَعُوٓا۟ أَصْوَٰتَكُمْ فَوْقَ صَوْتِ ٱلنَّبِىِّ وَلَا تَجْهَرُوا۟ لَهُۥ بِٱلْقَوْلِ كَجَهْرِ بَعْضِكُمْ لِبَعْضٍ أَن تَحْبَطَ أَعْمَـٰلُكُمْ وَأَنتُمْ لَا تَشْعُرُونَ ٢﴾

(سورة الحُجُرَات: ٢)

◖O you who believe! Raise not your voices above the voice of the Prophet, nor speak aloud to him in talk as you speak aloud to one another, lest your deeds should be rendered fruitless while you perceive not.◗ *(Qur'an: 49: 2)*

Showing good manners to the Prophet (ﷺ) is a fundamental part of Islamic law, in that those who do show good manners to him will be rewarded, while those who show bad manners to him will be punished. To honor the Prophet (ﷺ), to revere him, to hold him in high regard, and to give him the high level of respect that he deserves — these are all fundamental aspects of Islam. Each one of us should love the Prophet (ﷺ), without becoming guilty of going into excesses [as the Christians did by claiming that 'Eesa (ﷺ) possessed divine qualities] and without being negligent in our attitude towards him (which was the fault of those people of past nations who cursed, vilified, and even killed the Prophets that were sent to them). As Muslims, we must not object to anything the Prophet (ﷺ) did or said; instead, we must both accept and be pleased with every single one of his commands and prohibitions; furthermore, we must not feel about him the way we feel about other human beings by making the mistake of thinking that he was sometimes right, but was at other times wrong. Everything the Prophet (ﷺ) said was the truth, for he was divinely protected by Allah from being misguided. We must not be dry or indifferent towards the Prophet (ﷺ); and upon ascertaining the authenticity of one of his sayings, we must not reject that saying or have any doubt at all regarding it. We must not question the correctness of any of his judgments and rulings. And we must not put his sayings on the same level as sayings of leaders, kings, presidents, and emperors, for Allah raised him high above each of those groups of people and above all other created beings as well.

In fact, it is forbidden to say anything or do anything that involves even the least bit of disrespect towards the Prophet (ﷺ). If, as a Muslim, you are pleased with the Prophet (ﷺ) as a Messenger, if you believe in him, and if you follow him, you must honor him more than you honor any other person, and you must love him more that you love your children, your father, your own self, and all other people combined. You must believe in what he said, you must follow his commands, and you must stay away from his prohibitions. You must follow his Sunnah, you must be pleased with his rulings, and you must strive to follow him to the best of your ability. You must show respect and reverence to the Prophet's sayings. So when he or one of his sayings are mentioned, you should not laugh or raise your voice or act rudely in any other way; instead, you must pay close attention to anything that is said about him. Also, you must believe with certainty in all of his miracles, and you must strive to defend the honor of the Prophet (ﷺ), of the members of his household, and of his Companions.

﴿ ... فَٱلَّذِينَ ءَامَنُواْ بِهِۦ وَعَزَّرُوهُ وَنَصَرُوهُ وَٱتَّبَعُواْ ٱلنُّورَ ٱلَّذِىٓ أُنزِلَ مَعَهُۥٓ أُوْلَٰٓئِكَ هُمُ ٱلْمُفْلِحُونَ ۝ ﴾

(سورة الأعراف: ١٥٧)

﴿... So those who believe in him [Muhammad], honor him, help him, and follow the light [the Qur'an] which has been sent down with him, it is they who will be successful.﴾ *(Qur'an 7: 157)*

Therefore, each Muslim should do what the Companions did towards the Prophet (ﷺ), in terms of the manners they showed to him. When they would speak to him, they would speak with lowered voices; and when he would speak to them as a group, they remained still and attentive, as if birds were perched on their heads, and they feared that, if they moved only a little, the birds would fly away. And if one of them was walking along the road on his way to the Masjid and heard the Prophet (ﷺ) say from inside the Masjid, "O people, sit down,"[126] then that person would sit down right where he was on the pathway — such was the respect that the Companions showed to the Prophet (ﷺ). And if one of them had a child who rejected the sayings of the Prophet (ﷺ), then he (ﷺ) would make an oath never to speak to that child ever again. These are just a few of numerous examples which describe how the Prophet's Companions showed good manners towards the Prophet (ﷺ).

---

[126] Related by Abu Dâwood (1091) and al-Ḥâkim (1056), on the authority of Jâbir.

The Prophet:
A bearer of glad tidings

﴿وَبَشِّرِ ٱلْمُؤْمِنِينَ بِأَنَّ لَهُم مِّنَ ٱللَّهِ فَضْلًا كَبِيرًا ﴿٤٧﴾﴾   (سورة الأحزاب: ٤٧)

﴾And announce to the believers [in the Oneness of Allah and in His Messenger Muhammad] the glad tidings, that they will have from Allah a Great Bounty.﴿   *(Qur'an: 33: 47)*

The Prophet (ﷺ) said: "Give glad tidings (to people), and do not alienate or repel (them). Make matters easy, and do not make matters difficult."[127]

One of the most salient features of the Prophet's character was the fact that he was a bearer of glad tidings:

﴿يَٰٓأَيُّهَا ٱلنَّبِيُّ إِنَّآ أَرْسَلْنَٰكَ شَٰهِدًا وَمُبَشِّرًا وَنَذِيرًا ﴿٤٥﴾﴾(سورة الأحزاب: ٤٥)

﴾O Prophet [Muhammad]! Verily, We have sent to you as witness, and a bearer of glad tiding, and a warner.﴿   *(Qur'an: 33: 45)*

The Prophet (ﷺ) came with many glad tidings, with much news that was a cause of joy for mankind, the greatest of them being Faith in Allah. And what greater glad tidings could there have been than news about Allah? Prior to the advent of the Prophet (ﷺ), people lived in an era of darkness and disbelief. All that they knew was this world, and all that they had to look forward to was death and then, at least according to their beliefs,

---

[127] Related by Bukhari (69, 6125) and Muslim (1734), on the authority of Anas ibn Mâlik.

nothingness — no Paradise and no Hell-fire. So what great news it certainly was when the Prophet (ﷺ) came and told them that there was a life beyond this life, and that, if they obeyed their Lord, they could look forward to Paradise, which is as wide as are the heavens and the earth. And truly great were the glad tidings the Prophet (ﷺ) gave mankind about their Lord, informing them that their Lord was Merciful, Beneficent, and Oft-Forgiving. The Prophet (ﷺ) even gave glad tidings to those who sinned, for he informed them that, if they repented sincerely, their Lord would forgive them.

In fact, the vast majority of Islamic teachings involve glad tidings for mankind. The Prophet (ﷺ) gave glad tidings to the person who performs ablution, informing him that the act of performing ablution results in his sins being erased. The Prophet (ﷺ) informed Muslims that between one prayer and the next, and between one Ramaḍân and the next, and between one Ḥajj and the next, and between one 'Umrâh and the next a Muslim achieves absolution for his sins — with the exception of any major sins he may have committed. The Prophet (ﷺ) gave glad tidings to the blind, informing them that they would be rewarded for their affliction with Paradise. The Prophet (ﷺ) gave glad tidings to any parent who patiently endures the bereavement of his or her son, for the Prophet (ﷺ) said that such a parent will have a castle in Paradise. The Prophet (ﷺ) gave glad tidings to those who are ill, informing them that the suffering they endure results in their sins being erased. And the Prophet (ﷺ) gave glad tidings to the people who needed it the most, those who are afflicted with trials and tribulations, for he said that, if Allah wants good to befall a person (i.e. if Allah wants a person to achieve Paradise and rewards), then Allah afflicts him with trials and tribulations. The Prophet (ﷺ) gave glad tidings to those who, upon finishing one prayer, sit and wait for the next prayer to arrive: the Prophet (ﷺ) said that the angels send prayers upon such people and make supplications for them as long as they do not exit from the state of being pure. The Prophet (ﷺ) said that each time a person glorifies Allah, a date-palm tree will be planted for him in Paradise. And the Prophet (ﷺ) said that, when a person says one hundred times, "How perfect Allah is! And I praise Him," then his sins are removed from him even if (in quantity) they are like the foam of the ocean. The Prophet (ﷺ) also said that when a person commits a sin and then performs ablution, performs two units of prayer, and asks Allah for forgiveness, then Allah (ﷺ) forgives him. Sickness, anxiety, sadness, affliction, or even being pricked by a thorn — if any of these things befall a Muslim, then Allah will make those hardships an atonement for that person's sins.

And the Prophet (ﷺ) came with a noble and magnificent Book, a Book that gives believers who perform good deeds glad tidings of a goodly and handsome and generous reward. In that Book — the Noble Qur'an — Allah (ﷺ) forbade people from feeling a sense of hopeless:

(سورة يُوسُف: ٨٧) ﴾ ﴿ ٨٧ ﴾ وَلَا الْقَوْمُ الْكَفِرُونَ ﴿... إِنَّهُ لَا يَا يَتَأَسُّ مِن رَّوْحِ اللَّهِ إِلَّا﴿

﴾... Certainly no one despairs of Allah's Mercy, except the people who disbelieve.﴿
(Qur'an: 12: 87)

And Allah (ﷺ) forbade people from feeling a sense of despair:

(سورة الحِجر: ٥٦) ﴾ ﴿ ٥٦ ﴾ إِلَّا الضَّالُّونَ ﴿ وَقَالَ وَمَن يَقْنَطُ مِن رَّحْمَةِ رَبِّهِ

﴾And who despairs of the Mercy of his Lord except those who are astray?﴿
(Qur'an 15: 56)

Also, Allah (ﷺ) forbade people from becoming sad:

$$\{ \text{...} \, \textlinebreak وَلَا تَهِنُوا وَلَا تَحْزَنُوا \} \, (١٣٩)$$

(سورة آل عِمرَان: ١٣٩)

❨So do not become weak [against your enemy], nor be sad...❩

(Qur'an: 3: 139)

And what greater glad tidings can there be for sinners than the following verse:

$$\{ قُلْ يَـٰعِبَادِيَ الَّذِينَ أَسْرَفُوا عَلَىٰ أَنفُسِهِمْ لَا تَقْـنَطُوا مِن رَّحْمَةِ اللَّهِ إِنَّ اللَّهَ يَغْفِرُ الذُّنُوبَ جَمِيعًا إِنَّهُ هُوَ الْغَفُورُ الرَّحِيمُ (٥٣) \}$$

(سورة الزُّمَر: ٥٣)

❨Say, 'O *'ibâdi* [my slaves] who have transgressed against themselves [by committing evil deeds and sins]! Despair not of the mercy of Allah: verily Allah forgives all sins. Truly He is Oft-Forgiving, Most Merciful.❩

(Qur'an: 39: 53)

When the Prophet (ﷺ) sent messengers to distant lands — men whose job it would be to invite the inhabitants of those lands to Islam — he said to them: "Give glad tidings (to people), and do not alienate or repel (them). Make matters easy, and do not make matters difficult."

On another occasion, the Prophet (ﷺ) warned his Companions not to be harsh with others, since harshness has the effect of discouraging people from performing their Religious duties. The Prophet (ﷺ) said: "O people! Verily, among you are those who drive people away (from Islam and from worship by being harsh with them). When someone among you leads people (in Prayer), then let him shorten the length of his Prayer, for among the people are the elderly, the very young, the sick, and the ones who have important errands to perform."[128]

---

[128] Related by Bukhari (90, 702) and Muslim (466), on the authority of Abu Mas'ood.

The Prophet (ﷺ) often gave good news to others: He informed 'Â'ishah that Allah had declared her innocence; he told Ka'b ibn Mâlik (رضي الله عنه) that Allah accepted his repentance; he told Jâbir (رضي الله عنه) that Allah spoke to his father; he once gave Muslims in general glad tidings, informing them that Zayd (رضي الله عنه), Ja'far (رضي الله عنه) and Ibn Rawâhah (رضي الله عنه) were in Paradise; he informed Ubay ibn Ka'b (رضي الله عنه) that Allah mentioned him in the highest gathering of angels; he gave ten specific Companions glad tidings of Paradise; and he informed the people of Badr that Allah said to them, "Do what you want, for I have indeed forgiven you."[129] Furthermore, the Prophet (ﷺ) informed the Muslims who made a famous pledge underneath a tree that Allah was pleased with them; he told a person who prayed with him, and who had been the recipient of an Islamically decreed punishment, that Allah had forgiven him; and he told a man who constantly read chapter "Purity" of the Noble Qur'an that Allah (ﷻ) loved him. In short, the Prophet (ﷺ) was known for frequently conveying to others glad tidings and giving them cause to rejoice and be happy.

The Prophet, as a teacher

Allah (ﷻ) said:

﴿ ... وَأَنزَلَ ٱللَّهُ عَلَيْكَ ٱلْكِتَـٰبَ وَٱلْحِكْمَةَ وَعَلَّمَكَ مَا لَمْ تَكُن تَعْلَمُ وَكَانَ فَضْلُ ٱللَّهِ عَلَيْكَ عَظِيمًا ﴾ (١١٣)

(سورة النِّسَاء: ١١٣)

---

[129] Related by Bukhari (3007, 3983) and Muslim (2494), on the authority of 'Ali.

❲... Allah has sent down to you the Book [the Qur'an], and *al-Ḥikmah* [Islamic laws, knowledge of legal and illegal things, i.e. the Prophet's Sunnah — legal ways], and taught you that which you knew not. And Ever Great is the Grace of Allah unto you [O Muhammad].❳

(Qur'an 4: 113)

And in a hadith that is related in *Ṣaḥeeḥ Muslim*, the Messenger of Allah (ﷺ) said: "Whoever takes a path seeking knowledge, then, because of that, Allah makes easy for him a path to Paradise."[130]

Sent as a guide and an educator, the Prophet (ﷺ) taught Muslims everything they needed to know about their Religion — from the most important of beliefs, to fundamental aspects of worship, to the manners of a believer, to the minutest detail about the manners of eating and drinking.

When the Prophet (ﷺ) delivered a sermon, the hearts of his audience trembled with fear and awe. With his voice raised, with an angry expression on his face, and with red eyes, he seemed like a man who was warning his people about an impending attack by enemy forces. Due to the intensity of his tone, his sincerity, and the grave warnings he was giving about the Hereafter, the various members of his audience would either cry or feel regret for their sins, or both.

The Prophet's sermons were full of guidance and wisdom, such that they had the effect of increasing the Faith of the Companions. When someone would ask about a legal ruling, the Prophet (ﷺ), in his answer, would at once educate the questioner and tell him what would benefit him in his Religion. When someone asked for advice, the Prophet (ﷺ) replied with an answer

---

[130] Related by Muslim (2699), on the authority of Abu Hurayrah.

that filled the questioner's heart with Faith, piety, and righteousness. When the Prophet (ﷺ) used parables, analogies, or metaphors, he used palpable, easy-to-understand examples to make matters clear to his Companions. And when the Prophet (ﷺ) told stories of past Nations, he gained the full attention of his audience, at once captivating their hearts with beautiful stories and imparting to them important lessons.

But more than any other thing the Prophet (ﷺ) did, leading by example was by far the most effect teaching tool he had at his disposal. Every deed the Prophet (ﷺ) performed was noble and virtuous, and every deed he warned against and abstained from was evil and wicked. The entire Religion is founded on following the Prophet's example, and that is precisely what noble scholars and righteous Muslims have been doing for centuries.

The first word of revelation to ever descend upon the Prophet (ﷺ) was, "Read" — one of the strongest proofs and indications of the superiority of knowledge and the paramount importance of teaching and learning. Allah ordered the Prophet (ﷺ) to say: "O Allah, increase me in knowledge," but Allah (ﷺ) didn't order him to ask for an increase of any other thing. That is because knowledge is the path that leads to the good pleasure of Allah; it is the door that opens one up to a world of guidance, happiness, and success. Before ordering the Prophet (ﷺ) to say good words or perform good deeds, Allah (ﷺ) commanded him to gain knowledge:

(سورة محمّد: ١٩) ﴿... فَٱعۡلَمۡ أَنَّهُۥ لَآ إِلَٰهَ إِلَّا ٱللَّهُ ۝﴾

﴿So know [O Muhammad] that Lâ ilâha illa-Allâh [none has the right to be worshipped but Allah]...﴾ *(Qur'an 47: 19)*

The Messenger of Allah (ﷺ) said: "The example of what Allah sent me with, in terms of guidance and knowledge, is the example of (beneficial) rain (that falls from the sky and causes crops to grow)."[131] Knowledge is one of the main blessings Allah (ﷻ) bestowed upon the Prophet (ﷺ), and conveying knowledge is the greatest duty that Allah entrusted the Prophet (ﷺ) with:

﴿ ... وَيُعَلِّمُهُمُ ٱلْكِتَٰبَ وَٱلْحِكْمَةَ ... ﴿١٢٩﴾ ﴾   (سورة البَقَرَة: ١٢٩)

◆... And instruct them in the Book [this Qur'an] and *al-Ḥikmah* [full knowledge of Islamic laws and jurisprudence or wisdom or Prophethood, etc.]...◆   *(Qur'an 2: 129)*

The Prophet (ﷺ) fulfilled that duty, such that, from among his Companions, scores of fiqh jurists, *tafseer* scholars, preachers, educators, wise men, and hadith scholars graduated from his school of knowledge. It was those men that then carried on his mission, filling the world with knowledge, wisdom, light, and uprightness.

The Prophet (ﷺ) exhorted his Companions to spread the knowledge he conveyed to them. During one of the most important and famous of his sermons — which he delivered during the Farewell Pilgrimage — the Prophet (ﷺ) said: "And let the one who is present here convey (this message) to the one who is absent. For among those to whom my message is conveyed, there may be some who will understand (what I say) better than those who hear (what I say) firsthand."[132]

---

[131] Related by Bukhari (79) and Muslim (2282), on the authority of Abu Moosa al-Ash'ari.

[132] Related by Bukhari (1741, 7078) and Muslim (1679), on the authority of Abu Bakrah.

He also said: "May Allah make shine the one who hears my speech, memorizes it, stores it, and then conveys it, for there are many people who are like one who carries with him Fiqh (knowledge of Islam), taking it to one who has a higher level of understanding than he does."[133] And in yet another hadith, the Prophet (ﷺ) said: "Convey from me, even if it is a single verse."[134]

The Prophet's entire life was dedicated to educating the people of his Nation — teaching them how to pray, fast, give charity, perform Ḥajj, remember Allah, supplicate to Allah, eat, drink, and so on. He taught his Companions about all of these matters not all at once, but in stages, a little at a time:

(سورة الإسْراء: ١٠٦) ﴿وَقُرْءَانًا فَرَقْنَهُ لِتَقْرَأَهُ عَلَى ٱلنَّاسِ عَلَىٰ مُكْثٍ ... ۝﴾

{And [it is] a Qur'an which We have divided [into parts], in order that you might recite it to men at intervals...} *(Qur'an 17: 106)*

(سورة الفُرقان: ٣٢) ﴿وَقَالَ ٱلَّذِينَ كَفَرُوا لَوْلَا نُزِّلَ عَلَيْهِ ٱلْقُرْءَانُ جُمْلَةً وَٰحِدَةً كَذَٰلِكَ لِنُثَبِّتَ بِهِ فُؤَادَكَ وَرَتَّلْنَهُ تَرْتِيلًا ۝﴾

{And those who disbelieve say, 'Why is not the Qur'an revealed to him all at once?' Thus [it is sent down in parts], that We may strengthen your heart thereby. And We have revealed it to you gradually, in stages [It was revealed to the Prophet in 23 years].} *(Qur'an 25: 32)*

The Prophet (ﷺ) would prioritize his lessons, teaching his Companions (may Allah be pleased with them all) in order of

---

[133] Related by Tirmidhi (2658), on the authority of Ibn Mas'ood; refer also to *Kashf al-Khifâ* (2/423).

[134] Related by Bukhari (3461), on the authority of 'Abdullâh ibn 'Amr.

what was most important. And when he would give a lesson, he would repeat what he said, making sure his Companions fully grasped what he was teaching them. And when the Prophet (ﷺ) taught them a physical act of worship, he would perform it for them, so that they could watch him and then be better able to follow his teachings. It was in that light that the Prophet (ﷺ) said: "Pray as you have seen me pray,"[135] as well as, "Take from me your rites (of Ḥajj)";[136] or in other words, "Listen to what I say, observe what I do, and then do the same yourselves."

O Allah, send prayers and salutations upon the Prophet, upon his family, upon his Companions, and upon all those who follow his guidance until the Last Day.

---

[135] Related by Bukhari (631), on the authority of Mâlik ibn al-Ḥuwayrith.

[136] Related by Muslim (1297), on the authority of Jâbir ibn 'Abdullâh.